WHERE DO ALL THE CALCULATORS GO?

The Gospel According to Red Dwarf

By Steve Trower

Copyright © Steve Trower 2022

No part of this book may be reproduced in any form, by photocopying or by any electronic or mechanical means, including information storage or retrieval systems, without permission in writing from both the copyright owner and the publisher of this book.

Red Dwarf by Grant Naylor Productions
© BBC & UKTV 1988-2020

Scripture quotations marked NIV are from THE HOLY BIBLE, NEW INTERNATIONAL VERSION ®, NIV ® Copyright © 1973, 1978, 1984, 2011 by Biblica, Inc. ® Used by permission. All rights reserved worldwide.

Scripture quotations marked NLV are taken from the New Life Version, copyright © 1969 and 2003. Used by permission of Barbour Publishing, Inc., Uhrichsville, Ohio 44683. All rights reserved.

Scripture quotations marked MSG are taken from THE MESSAGE, copyright © 1993, 2002, 2018 by Eugene H. Peterson. Used by permission of NavPress. All rights reserved. Represented by Tyndale House Publishers, Inc.

Scripture quotations marked NLT are taken from the Holy Bible, New Living Translation, copyright © 1996, 2004, 2015 by Tyndale House Foundation. Used by permission of Tyndale House Publishers, Inc., Carol Stream, Illinois 60188. All rights reserved.

Scripture quotations marked NCV taken from the New Century Version®. Copyright © 2005 by Thomas Nelson. Used by permission. All rights reserved.

Scripture quotations marked VOICE taken from The Voice™. Copyright © 2008 by Ecclesia Bible Society. Used by permission. All rights reserved.

Scripture quotations marked GW taken from GOD'S WORD®. © 1995, 2003, 2013, 2014, 2019, 2020 by God's Word to the Nations Mission Society. Used by permission.

Also by Steve Trower

The Ballad of Matthew Smith

The Ambivalence Chronicles –
a Sci-fi Comedy in 8 Bits:
Bit#1: The Chip Whisperer
Bit#2: The Kempston Interface
Bit#3: The Road Worrier

Countless as the Stars

www.stevetrower.co.uk
twitter.com/SPTrowerEsq

To my darling Candy.

All characters portrayed within this book are fictitious and any resemblance to persons living or dead is purely coincidental.

Contents

The End: An Introduction	11
Part One: The Gospel According to Red Dwarf	17
The Gospel According to Dave	19
The Gospel According to Rimmer	43
The Gospel According to Cat	71
The Gospel According to Kryten	83
Part Two: The Triple Fried Egg Chilli Chutney Sandwich and other parables	105
The Triple Fried Egg Chilli Chutney Sandwich	107
Justice	113
Time Travelly Paradoxy Sci-fi Smeg	124
Backwards	132
A four-course meal of fear, vanity, guilt, and anger	135
Blubbery Schoolgirl Mush	142
I think I E5 A9 08 B7 you	150
If we're not who we thought we were, who the hell are we?	153
Your Father is Dad	155

More than just a toaster	159
Demons & Angels	163
The Beginning: Better Then Life	169

The End: an Introduction

Three million years from Earth, the mining ship Red Dwarf. Its crew: Dave Lister, the last human being alive; Arnold Rimmer, a hologram of his dead bunkmate; and a creature who evolved from the ship's cat.

The chances are, if you're reading this, you already have at least a passing familiarity with the Jupiter Mining Ship Red Dwarf. And that being the case, you might be wondering where I'm hoping to find something vaguely resembling a Gospel message in the largely nihilistic universe of Red Dwarf. And I wouldn't blame you; frankly, at this stage, I am wondering that myself.

The fact that Red Dwarf is both science fiction and comedy means that a lot of frankly ridiculous stuff happens. I've tried to carry a similar sense of humour through this book, but the subject matter occasionally requires me to take these ridiculous events more seriously than they were intended. Let me assure you this doesn't mean I missed the joke.

Another non-trivial problem is that Red Dwarf has been running for 11 series and 2 feature length specials spanning more than 30 years, which in themselves have a somewhat sketchy sense of continuity, without getting into the four novels (the last two of which both follow on directly from the second, but in different universes). For the sake of simplicity, we won't involve the novels here; even without them, there is plenty of material to work with.

So before we embark on this three million year odyssey, here's a quick reminder of the bigger picture; a brief overview of what religion looks like in the Red Dwarf universe. As a starting point, take Holly's opening monologue from the beginning of series 2:

> *As the days go by, we face the increasing inevitability that we are alone in a godless, uninhabited, hostile and meaningless universe. Still, you've got to laugh, haven't you?*

Three million years without meeting a single Christian, Muslim, Buddhist or Pastafarian could perhaps lead an artificial intelligence with an IQ of 6,000 to this conclusion, and while this is the primary worldview of the series, various religious systems do exist within the Dwarf universe.

Religions with apparent pseudo-Christian roots have developed within Cat culture, and been programmed into mechanoids, calculators and other electronic devices (except cheap toasters), along with the certain knowledge that 'human heaven' was just made up to stop us all going mad.

Meanwhile, Humanity itself has developed into a culture which thinks a dedication could form part of the holy scriptures, and in which Christianity has devolved into weird cultish sects like the Seventh Day Advent Hoppists and the Church of Judas – both of which claim the Rimmer family as one-time members.

This almost certainly contributed to Rimmer rejecting the idea of God as preposterous, despite at the same time holding a completely unfounded faith in a species of aliens he made up, and a belief in reincarnation – specifically that in a past life he was Alexander the Great's Chief Eunuch. This strange mish-mash of beliefs is somewhat reminiscent of 21st Century spirituality, a sort of post-modern cherry picking of whatever elements fit in with our pre-conceived ideals.

None of which stops Rimmer from being a complete smeghead, of course.

Interestingly, despite the existence of these complex and often deeply held beliefs, the only person we see actively discussing matters of faith and philosophy throughout most of Red Dwarf is Lister – who was described in Back to Reality as 'the ultimate atheist', but would prefer to consider himself a pantheist (not a frying pantheist though - those guys are weird).

In practice, Lister doesn't seem to follow a specific belief system, but he frequently demonstrates an awareness of the story of Jesus, and a strong sense of personal morality (especially in contrast to Rimmer's complete lack of the same).

The first part of this book – the 'gospels' – will look in more detail at the experiences and worldviews of the four main characters, and how they reflect what the Bible says.

In part two we change the pace slightly, with a collection of shorter articles highlighting various themes which have been covered in Red Dwarf over the years. Jesus often used everyday experiences in parables to highlight a deeper truth; my parables take events from Red Dwarf to give a fresh angle on what the Bible says about such things as love, justice, identity, and temporal mechanics.

*

Throughout the book I have quoted passages from various Bible translations. For clarity I have primarily used the New International Version, but occasionally I've quoted other translations where they better illustrate the point I'm trying to make.

This isn't an attempt to change what the Bible says, just to make sure the emphasis of the specific quote helps to clarify the point I'm making (or sometimes because it contrasts nicely with a line from Red Dwarf). While the wording of specific sentences may vary between translations, the meaning is the same, especially when read in the context of a longer passage – which I definitely recommend. The longer passages are freely available in numerous translations at biblegateway.com if you want to check my work.

With all that in mind, I should point out that I'm not a theologian in any way; I'm just a guy who reads the Bible and watches Red Dwarf, and one day got a crazy idea to mash the two together and see what happened. So if you think I've got it wrong anywhere, just remember: *the hats were supposed to be green.*

Now, let us embark upon our potentially pointless mission to salvage Biblical truth from the depressing wastes of deep space – beginning, appropriately, with a single human being, alone in the universe.

PART ONE

THE GOSPEL ACCORDING TO RED DWARF

THE GOSPEL ACCORDING TO DAVE

If You're God, Why That Face?

In the beginning was The End, and in The End was Lister, and Lister was God.

The End (Series 1, Episode 1) not only takes on the task of introducing the hero (Lister) and killing his nemesis (Rimmer), it then goes on to evolve a pregnant cat into a sentient humanoid, and introduces us to a Cat civilisation every bit as complex as our own, even featuring its own set of contentious religious beliefs. When Lister casually mentions Frankenstein, Cat is reminded how he learnt in Kitty School about

> the Holy Mother, saved by Cloister the Stupid, who was frozen in time, and who gaveth of his life that we might live; who shall returneth to lead us to Fuchal, the Promised Land.

In the script it's just a throwaway line to set Lister back in pursuit of his Fijian dream – we all need a purpose in this increasingly nihilistic universe, right? – but from this line that Cat once learned by rote, we see that Lister has become a sort of Messiah to the Cat people.

Obviously no deity in its right mind would make Dave Lister any kind of Chosen One; in human terms he was nothing: a Liverpudlian art college drop-out of dubious parentage, found abandoned under the pool table in the

Aigburth Arms as an infant. Lazy, uncouth, and insubordinate, he got a job fixing the dispensing machines on board Red Dwarf, but remained the lowest ranked member of the crew, reporting to the hopelessly inept Second Technician Rimmer.

And yet, from the lowliest imaginable birth, to growing up in an undesirable neighbourhood, to taking a very ordinary, working class job; and despite not caring much for appearances, ambition, or material wealth, Lister willingly handed himself over, forfeiting several months life and pay, rather than have his cat put down.

Now, switch out 23rd Century Liverpool for 1st Century Galilee, and we find another unlikely 'Chosen One'. In human terms, he was nothing: a child of dubious parentage, born in a feeding trough behind an inn and brought up as a carpenter (Mark 6:3) in the unfashionable end of Nazareth, he eventually chose the life of a traveller, roaming from town to town, mixing with the unloved, unwanted and dishonest, with nothing to call his own but his shoes and his friends. Like Lister, he had no beauty or majesty to attract us to him, nothing in his appearance that we should desire him (Isa 53:2); in human terms, Jesus was a nobody.

And yet... from the lowliest imaginable birth, to growing up in an undesirable neighbourhood, to taking a very ordinary, working class job; and despite not caring much for appearances, ambition, or material wealth (Matt 6:25-34), Jesus willingly handed himself over, forfeiting his own life, so that we can live.

Lister's incarnation as Cloister is, unsurprisingly, an imperfect analogy for Christ, but has the potential to present us with a very human face of God: ill-equipped for a job he doesn't want, and all but forgotten by those he gave his life to save.

To the viewer, Lister serves another purpose. This is, after all, science fiction, and science fiction often needs something to connect it to the real world. That's why the Doctor usually travels with a 20th Century human, why Arthur Dent was saved from the Vogons, and why Buck Rogers woke up 500 years in the future. They provide us with something familiar, an everyman, a viewpoint we can all relate to in an otherwise unfamiliar world. Dave Lister, a working class lad from Liverpool stuck in deep space and the distant future, bridges the gap for us between the ordinary and the extraordinary.

And just as Lister is our bridge to Red Dwarf, Jesus is our link to the throne room of heaven. By stepping down from the extraordinary and living a life every bit as ordinary as ours, facing the kind of every day trials we do, Jesus gives us a chance to witness the fantastic.

That is why that face.

You're him off the Bible aren't you?

– Rimmer, Lemons

I'm not a god – I've just been misquoted!

Over the years it has been a common argument against Christianity that Jesus never actually claimed to be God. And from a purely pedantic perspective, that time when Jesus pulled the apostles aside and said, 'Listen chaps, I know some of you have figured this out already, but for the avoidance of doubt, I am actually God', has indeed been lost in translation somewhere.

Lister, on the other hand, after his initial, somewhat surprised exclamation that 'I am your God!' soon settles on a much more realistic viewpoint and actively denies being any kind of god:

> *I'm not a god – I've just been misquoted!*
> *– Lister, Waiting For God*

And indeed he has: after thousands of years of war over the colour of their hats, half the cat people set off for Fuchal following what turned out to be Lister's laundry list, and flew straight into an asteroid.

We might like to think that as Christians we're too smart to mistake something as benign as a laundry list for the ultimate guide to our destiny; yet we sometimes overlook the fact that the Bible literally includes laundry lists (Lev 13:47-59), and other segments which served a purpose at the time they were written, but which no longer apply in 21st Century western civilisation. Like those luckless cat people, we can get so caught up in trying to follow what we think the scriptures are telling us that we don't notice the giant meteor that reality has placed in our path.

Now, before anyone wonders if I'm one of those who likes to pick and choose which parts of the Bible I follow, consider this: We might like to think that we wouldn't be so petty as to squabble amongst ourselves over whether the hats should be red or blue, but I'm sure God looks down at us sometimes and thinks much the same as Lister did:

> *They were supposed to be green!*
> *— Lister, Waiting for God*

So if you're a Christian and come across something in this book that you don't agree with, or that doesn't quite fit your beliefs, that's ok. As long as we're both following Christ the best way we know how, and don't go starting wars with each other for no very good reason, it doesn't matter if we don't agree on every little point.

We're probably both wrong anyway.

*

Cloister the Stupid wasn't that bothered that two factions disagreed on a minor point; he didn't even care that they were all wrong. What bothered him was this:

> *They're just using religion as an excuse to be extremely crappy to each other.*
>   *– Lister, Waiting for God*

And this issue of bad things being done in the name of religion – specifically, in the name of Jesus – comes up again in *Lemons* (S10 E3). Here, the crew encounter Jesus in first Century India and bring him back to Red Dwarf, where he discovers that he will start Christianity, and through it, seemingly become responsible for the Crusades and the Westboro Baptists. Understandably horrified at this prospect, Jesus returns to his own time and immediately sets about trashing his reputation in order to prevent Christianity from ever existing.

In the end, this all transpires to be a simple case of mistaken identity, for the boys have encountered Jesus of Caesarea, inventor of the carrier bag, and not the more famous one from Nazareth.

Unlike his namesake, the Nazarene did not need to visit the far future to see what would be done in his name; being in nature God (Phil 2:6) he already had access to knowledge of everything that would follow, good and bad. He could also have easily avoided his human fate – he could have mule-kicked the guy on the left, clobbered the one on the right, and been over that green hill and far away before you could say 'Pontius Pilate'; or indeed just slipped away to India and never gone back to Jerusalem.

But he didn't.

Even with divine knowledge of every way his words would be twisted or misinterpreted or ignored, he just went right ahead and said them.

Fully aware of every death that would be caused 'in his name' but against his wishes, he went on as planned.

Even knowing the cup of suffering that lay in his path if he carried on, he accepted his destiny, lived his life as the Son of Man, and died the death of the King of the Jews.

And he did that because he also knew the good that would be done in his name. He knew that eventually his followers would bring about improvements to health and schooling throughout the world. He knew that his followers would eventually abolish slavery as a legitimate trade. He allowed himself to be crucified because the needs of the many outweigh the needs of- wait, no, wrong franchise. He allowed himself to be crucified because by that act, we – *you* – can be forgiven and granted eternal life.

He went through with the plan because, although some stupid people would do some stupid things in his name, the good would far outweigh the bad.

Last Human

Through no fault of his own, Dave Lister has become the last human being in the universe, but he is never quite as alone as in *M-Corp* (S12 E5), when news of the Jupiter Mining Corporation's acquisition by an all-powerful conglomerate finally reaches Red Dwarf.

Following M-Corp's takeover of Red Dwarf they install a perception filter, which prevents Lister from being able to see or hear anything not provided by the corporation – including his crewmates.

As the Red Dwarf Posse fade from his perception, Lister is forced to trade his life for stuff he doesn't really need, until he ends up trapped at M-Corp, surrounded by a succession of false friends, but feeling more alone than at any time in the last thirty years.

Thanks to future science, Kryten is able to free both Lister and Red Dwarf from M-Corp's influence by rebooting them and restoring their last safe settings:

> *We need to reinstall your personality; we have to delete everything and reinstall new files.*
> *– Kryten, M-Corp*

And on those occasions when the constant need to get more stuff or new 'friends' feels like it's sapping your life, the answer is surprisingly similar:

> *Do not conform to the pattern of this world, but be transformed by the renewing of your mind.*
> *Rom 12:2 (NIV)*

This is not a single reboot, however, but a continuing process of transformation that starts with encountering Jesus, and goes on as we dedicate ourselves, body and mind, to his wishes.

*

Of course, Lister has never really been alone; Holly – Red Dwarf's tenth generation AI hologramatic computer with an IQ of 6,000 – has been Lister's omnipotent protector from the beginning, keeping him safe in stasis until the radiation levels on board Red Dwarf were safe, and thereafter taking on the duties of keeping him alive, and sane, and if at all possible returning him safely home.

> *My job is to keep Dave sane. True, I'm not that good at it, but I do my best. That's why I create these little diversions to keep him occupied.*
> *– Holly, Back in the Red Part 3*

Holly also recognises that it is not good for Lister to be alone (Gen 2:18), and so (not realising that there's a perfectly good Felis sapiens lurking in the ship somewhere) Holly creates a hologram – a virtual crewmate – to prevent Lister from going space crazy through loneliness.

In Holly's near infinite wisdom, he knows that what Lister needs to keep him sane and alive 3 million years from Earth is not a girlfriend, or a drinking buddy, as Lister might have chosen, but Second Technician Arnold Rimmer. As bunkmates before the accident, Rimmer was the crew member who knew Lister best; they may not have actually liked each other, but as Jean Paul Sartre said, hell is being locked forever in a room with your friends.

The wisdom of Holly's choice starts to become clear in the unmade Series 1 script *Bodysnatcher*, in which Lister inadvertently sets the sleeping quarters on fire and turns to Rimmer, who even in hologramatic form saves him from destroying Red Dwarf. It's funny how we sometimes need to burn our metaphorical spaceship before we'll accept that maybe the all-knowing Holly who looks out for us actually does know best…

Just how reliant Lister and the crew are on Holly is brought to the fore in *White Hole* (S4 E4), when Holly's intelligence is increased exponentially at the cost of her run time, causing her to shut down, taking with her the engines, navigation and all but emergency power. Everything, in fact, except the oxygen recycler, minimal heating and lighting… and Rimmer.

As well as maintaining Lister's mental and emotional stability, Holly has been keeping him physically safe, effectively keeping his world running, and when Holly shuts down, the crew suddenly finds out what happens when the entity that provides them with food, warmth, and the air they breathe is suddenly taken out of the equation:

> *It leaves us galloping up diarrhoea drive without a saddle.*
> *– Kryten, White Hole*

Just as Holly's ongoing mission is to ensure the survival of the human race through Lister, God takes care of the whole human race by treating each of us as if we were the only human.

> *The life I now live in the body, I live by faith in the Son of God, who loved me and gave himself for me.*
> *Gal 2:20 NIV*

> *In the same way, there is joy in the presence of God's angels when even one sinner repents.*
> *Luke 15:10 NLT*

God's care and protection is just as personal as Holly's is for Lister; the difference being that God's runtime is infinite, and he will never shut himself down and leave us to fend for ourselves.

Humans, however, are much more fickle; for the Red Dwarf Posse, this shows through their suggesting that Holly has gone a bit senile and started making mistakes.

In *Queeg* (S2 E5) a mysterious subroutine decides that Holly has endangered the crew, and the backup computer, Queeg, is activated.

Queeg is quick to enforce the rules, and soon has Cat and Lister scrubbing floors to earn their food, and enforces physical training and revision schedules for Rimmer, while Holly is confined to a cathode ray tube and demoted to the role of night watchman.

Holly may seem to have gone a bit peculiar at times, but as he bids the team farewell, he shows a pretty good understanding of Rimmer's rather shallow outlook on life:

> *I hope you meet those aliens you're looking for who can give you a body, and you become an officer and you get a sex life, and all the other millions of things you feel you need to make you happy.*
>   *– Holly, Queeg*

Pretty accurate for an apparently senile artificial intelligence; yet despite Holly demonstrating this level of understanding and that he does, in fact, know what's best for the crew, they carry on in blissful ignorance, failing to defend Holly as Queeg takes control of Red Dwarf.

Like intergalactic Israelites lost in the wilderness of space, the tribe of Red Dwarf forsake their benevolent protector for whatever alternative comes along (Ex 32:1-8). Unfortunately for them, Queeg lacks Holly's grace (denying Rimmer his unnecessary four hour lie-in) and mercy (rigidly enforcing cleaning duties, despite their effect on Cat's cuticles).

And let's face it, Holly would have every right to behave that way, to be a cruel leader, all stick and no carrot. The fact that he doesn't give the crew what they deserve (most of the time) isn't a sign that he's computer senile – it's because he's a really good bloke.

Likewise, God has every right to be hard on us. A lot of the time we don't exactly treat his creation with a lot of respect; we slob around, making a mess of the place and when the smeg hits the fan we expect God to send his skutters along to sort our mess out. And most of the time, he tolerates that.

Most of the time, he just wants to be one of the crew for our journey home – sure, he's the one ultimately in control, but he'll allow us our little diversions, our four hour lie-ins and refusal to clean up after ourselves.

Like Holly, God likes having us around, despite our flaws – but, like Holly, when we start to take advantage, or he finds our lack of faith disturbing, he'll break out his hidden Queeg and bring us back into line the hard way.

To Find Your Creator

It's not an easy thing, to find your creator.
– Rimmer, Back to Earth part 3

In *Back To Earth*, our heroes are sent through a dimensional portal, where they discover they are from an 'invalid dimension'; worse still, in the nearest valid dimension they are just characters in a TV show, destined to die at the end of the three-part special currently being filmed.

Despite apparently accepting that – in this reality at least – they are fictional characters, the boys take exception to the idea of just being killed off, and head off in search of their Creator to beg for an extension, or a spin-off, or anything other than oblivion…

This part of the story is a direct parody of *Blade Runner* – a movie which itself explores what it means to be human – and so we find our heroes searching for answers, looking for meaning in a world they were never meant to inhabit.

> *We need answers, like, "How many episodes do we have left?"*
> — Kryten, BTE3

That might not be the question most of us are asking, but the journey, the search for a home, for our true identity, and hopefully the discovery that something other than oblivion awaits when we run out of episodes... This is the spiritual journey that awaits us all.

For Lister, it starts with discovering his true self – which, unfortunately, is a soap actor in recovery for drug addiction.

> *The guy's a wreck. He pretends to be somebody else all day.*
> — Lister, BTE 3

Although this seems like a disappointing start for the boys from the Dwarf, it is where we all begin our journeys. We may not be a drug addict or a soap actor, but we're all hiding some iniquity, pretending to be better than we are. On some level, we're all a wreck in the beginning, dead because of our failures and sins (Eph 2:1). Discovering his inner wreck is the first step on Lister's quest to find the Creator.

To the Dwarfers, in this new reality, the Creator is more than a writer: he has become a god. Armed only with a typewriter, he wields unlimited power; what he types into the lives of the crew, must come to pass. Although Lister's initial intention is fairly shallow – he wants more life – along the way he has reevaluated his life:

> *I've been dead for ages, man – just sitting around, getting old and fat. I never thought I had responsibility to anyone. I never thought there was anyone out there who was on my side, who wanted things to work out. We've got a fan club. They've even named a TV station after me. I was never alone, I just didn't realise it. Now I want more life, smegger!*
> *– Lister, BTE 3*

We too can sit around, dead in our sins, getting old and fat, pretending we have no responsibilities. But you have a fan club. God is on your side, not just wanting things to work out, but making them work out:

> *We know that God makes all things work together for the good of those who love Him and are chosen to be a part of His plan.*
> *Rom 8:28 (NLV)*

You may not have your name on a TV station, but it's written in heaven, and in the Book of Life:

> *Rejoice that your names are written in heaven!*
> *Luke 10:20 (VOICE)*

> *Conquerors will march in the victory parade, their names indelible in the Book of Life.*
> *Rev 3:5 (MSG)*

And above all this, you can have more life – and not just a third rate sitcom, but life to the fullest:

> *I came to give life – life in all its fullness.*
> *John 10:10 (NCV)*

All you have to do is find your creator – thankfully easier than Rimmer makes out:

> *God wanted them to look for him and perhaps search all around for him and find him, though he is not far from any of us.*
> *Acts 17:27 (NCV)*

*

The last minute plot twist comes when Lister inadvertently kills his own creator. Suddenly our heroes find themselves freed from mindlessly doing the will of the Creator, and try to write their own ending:

> *Hey, man, I feel like a god! I feel like I've got liquid gold coursing through every vein in my body. Hey, we can get out of this. As long as we've got this, we control the world. We can do whatever we want.*
> *– Lister, BTE3*

It's easy to be tempted by that way of thinking; being god of our own lives, having control of our own little piece of the world, and having the freedom and power to do whatever we want is a very seductive idea.

Lister lets this new found power go to his head, inflicting unnecessary pain and humiliation on Rimmer; and even once Kryten figures out that they are not actually in control of their destinies, Lister is torn between the comatose dream of life with Kochanski, and a full life on board Red Dwarf.

Luckily, our creator isn't some capricious writer liable to get bored of us and move on to something new at any moment.

> *I grew weary of you.*
> *– The Creator, BTE3*

> *Keep your lives free from the love of money. Be happy with what you have. God has said, "I will never leave you or let you be alone."*
> *Heb 13:5 (NLV)*

And while we did inadvertently kill our creator, his death freed us from our lust, greed, and hunger for power, and left us the option to choose between reality with him, or without.

And the moral of the story is:

Appreciate what you've got, because basically, I'm fantastic!

– Holly, Queeg

Be happy with what you have. God has said, "I will never leave you or let you be alone."

Heb 13:5 (NLV)

THE GOSPEL ACCORDING TO RIMMER

Death isn't the handicap it used to be!

One of the first sci-fi principles we are introduced to in the Red Dwarf universe is the ability to retain a deceased crew member's knowledge and experience in the form of a hologram.

On screen, Holly is only able to sustain one hologram, and the first crew member to die on the mission is George McIntyre, someone further up Rimmer's chain of command but not critical to the mission, prompting his 'welcome back' speech:

> *My advice to anyone more vital to the mission than me is: if you die, I'll kill you.*

Ordinarily, Second Technician Rimmer would not be troubling this particular directive, but three million years from Earth, Red Dwarf's mission has changed, and as the crew member best suited to keeping the last human alive and sane, Rimmer finds himself elevated to the rank of ship's hologram.

But Rimmer, despite having been granted a potentially eternal – if physically restricted – second chance at life, remains unconvinced that this is altogether a positive thing. Indeed, the question of whether or not a digital replica of a person is that person, appears to be bothering him, despite Lister's assurances that

> *Death isn't the handicap it used to be.*

This may be easy to say if you've outlived the rest of your species by a couple of ice ages, but for Rimmer, his new hologramatic existence seems only to add to his list of personal inadequacies.

This is why he makes it his personal mission to somehow make himself whole again; to create, borrow or steal himself a real, solid, living body.

The first chance he gets to try this is in *Bodyswap* (S3 E4), after Lister inadvertently tries to destroy Red Dwarf with a milkshake and a Toffee Crisp. The crew's attempt to not get blown up leads them to upload a dead senior officer's mind into Lister's body to shut down the auto-destruct; this in turn leads Rimmer to realise that he and Lister can likewise trade minds, effectively loaning Lister's body to Rimmer on the basis that he has the self-discipline needed to help get it back into shape.

Obviously there is no evidence that Rimmer can or will do this, or that he deserves this body swap in any way. Yet, thanks to Lister's inexplicable generosity, he is given that opportunity; an opportunity not just to exercise, but to eat, to touch, to unpack Rachel and get the puncture repair kit… Rimmer is gifted this chance at what is, from his perspective, a much better life – a real, physical body, at least for a fortnight every summer – but by lying, cheating, and general selfishness, he manages to screw it up.

The same opportunity is offered to each of us – a fuller life, as different from the one we know as our lives are from that of a hologram with no physical presence – and likewise offered out of undeserved generosity. But the offer open to us is for more than a couple of weeks; it's for life in all its fullness, starting now and lasting forever. All we have to do is accept it graciously, and not be a smeghead.

And when we do that, death really isn't the handicap it used to be.

> Then, when our dying bodies have been transformed into bodies that will never die, this Scripture will be fulfilled:
> "Death is swallowed up in victory.
> O death, where is your victory?
> O death, where is your sting?"
> 1 Cor 15:54-55 (NLT)

That's why the apostle Paul wrote that to die is gain – 'Life versus even more life!' (Phil 1:21 [MSG])

Faith, hop and charity, and the greatest of these is hop.

– Rimmer, The Last Day

And now these three remain: faith, hope and love. But the greatest of these is love.

1 Cor 13:13 (NIV)

If you don't have rules, what are you left with?

No right thinking individual would argue that sensible rules, properly enforced, don't form the basis of a well-adjusted society. But as we see from the very beginning, Rimmer is not the most right thinking of individuals, and has something of an obsession with 'The Rules'.

And that obsession doesn't change once he becomes a hologram: in the unmade episode *Bodysnatcher*, three million years after an explosion wipes out everyone but Lister, Rimmer decides it is necessary to hold a roll call to establish the extent of casualties.

This is ridiculously legalistic, but for Rimmer, following the rules is a way of hanging on to some shred of normality.

The problem here is not that Rimmer wants to follow the rules; it's that he wants to follow the rules at the expense of everything else. What started out as respect for the rules has become so blinkered it leaves no room for adaptation when circumstances have changed way beyond the need for the original rules; in this case, rules laid down three million years ago, to manage hundreds of people following a specific mission within a large organisation.

We can all see that what is really needed in this scenario is not rigid adherence to irrelevant rules, but compassion for the remaining crew member as he grieves everyone he ever knew. Surely it's ok to change or even discard certain rules when the world in which they are being applied has changed in a way the rule makers could never have foreseen?

Rules are not created in a vacuum. There must have been some circumstance, unknown to us as outsiders, which gave rise to Space Corps Directive 5796 ('No officer above the rank of mess sergeant is permitted to go into combat with pierced nipples'), but without that context it's just a meaningless rule, the benefit of which remains a mystery.

It was this kind of obsession with rules at the expense of all else that brought Jesus into conflict with the Pharisees (Matt 12:1-14):

> One Sabbath, Jesus was strolling with his disciples through a field of ripe grain. Hungry, the disciples were pulling off the heads of grain and munching on them. Some Pharisees reported them to Jesus: "Your disciples are breaking the Sabbath rules!"
> Matt 12:1-2 (MSG)

The Pharisees were very much the Rimmers of the first century Jews in this respect, strutting around with their clipboards and memorised Space Corps Directives, desperate to catch Jesus and his mates in some trivial act of rebellion just to put them on report, miladdo.

For them, like Rimmer, the rules were everything; every last sub-clause had to be followed to the letter, and it was Jesus' refusal to acknowledge their increasingly petty rules that rubbed them up the wrong way.

But Jesus wasn't doing this out of some Lister-esque one-upmanship, or because rules aren't important; the fact is that the Pharisees had created a raft of unnecessary 'extra' rules and treated them as equal to the Scriptures. Like Rimmer's superfluous roll-call, they ended up contradicting the intended purpose of rules.

> By your own rules, which you teach people, you are rejecting what God said. And you do many things like that.
> Mark 7:13 (NCV)

The Rimmers of the world will tend to see God as making demands of us, caring only that we keep the rules. What Jesus did, and what Christians should seek to do, is to look beyond the letter of the law, and see what God really wants from us.

For example, Space Corps Directive 597 states that quarantine bays are provided one berth per registered crew member. Rimmer, high on power and crazed by a hex virus, interprets this literally, and because neither Cat nor Kryten are on the official crew manifest, they end up sharing Lister's bunk for the duration of their quarantine. On the face of it, Directive 597 is a perfectly sensible rule, not least for preventing cross-contamination. But as we can see in *Quarantine* (S5 E4), not only is it irrelevant where the quarantine bays outnumber the crew, but it causes more harm by setting them at each other's throats.

Even when not insane and egged on by Mr Flibble, Rimmer fails to see this.

Clearly Rimmer has, on more than one occasion, taken legalism to a literal extreme. Maybe we can trace the reason for this back to his upbringing; Rimmer's family were, apparently, Seventh Day Advent Hoppists – an obscure religious sect whose legalistic interpretation of an already dubious Bible translation ('Faith, hop and charity, and the greatest of these is hop.') should surely be its own argument against literalism.

Now I'm not saying we can just overlook bits of the Bible because they 'don't sound right', but I do believe that some rules are no longer useful. If you can count the remaining crew on one finger, a roll call is clearly a waste of time. Similarly, enjoying a full English breakfast is certainly not top of my list of 'Things to repent'. (Lev 11:7; 17:10)

Which begs the question: why are the rules still there? Especially with the existence of the more Rimmery fringe who will throw certain Levitical rules at people while wiping scampi from their face on their polycotton sleeves. (Lev 11:9-11; 19:19)

Well, the Old Testament law consists of ceremonial, cultural and moral laws. To enlightened 21st Century Christians there is obviously a difference; things like keeping your dangerous ox secure and not sleeping with your sister-in-law have a timeless moral relevance, whereas what hairstyles and tattoos you can and cannot have is, within reason, usually considered a matter of personal choice.

That said, this difference is not always explicit within the Old Testament text, nor is it made in any New Testament references to the law. James even goes so far as to say the opposite:

> *If you obey all the Laws but one, you are as guilty as the one who has broken them all.*
> *James 2:10 (NLV)*

Based on which, doing a Sunday shift in Asda to pay your mortgage, or going to church with a pimple, are on a par with killing Bob next door and stealing his lawnmower.

But…

God isn't lurking round every corner with his clipboard waiting to catch us out. Unlike Space Corps Directives, the Law isn't meant to be followed. Even as he dictated them to Moses, God knew that it was not humanly possible to keep every one. To try and do so is to misunderstand their purpose: to highlight the fallen nature of man, and our need for salvation.

> Sir, the Space Corps directives are there to protect us. They are not a set of vindictive pronouncements directed against any one person.
> – Kryten, Quarantine

God didn't send Rimmer and his abused copy of the Space Corps Directives manual to make sure we earn our way to heaven; he sent Jesus, precisely because we can't earn our way into heaven.

The Pharisees, like Rimmer, obsessed over every little rule so much that they overlooked the heart behind the rules, which Jesus summed up in like this:

> Love the Lord your God with all your heart and with all your soul and with all your mind. This is the first and greatest commandment. And the second is like it: Love your neighbour as yourself. All the Law and the Prophets hang on these two commandments.
> Matt 22:37-40 (NIV)

Jesus showed that love and compassion is better than blind legalism; they don't go out of date as readily either.

If you don't have rules, what are you left with? Grace.

One of yous has gotta go.

> *This can't go on. One of yous has gotta go.*
> *— Lister, Me²*

Late in series 1 Lister, aided by a hallucination caused by a mutated pneumonia virus, works out that if they shut down all non-essential systems, Holly would be able to support more than one hologram – theoretically Rimmer and Kochanski. However, Rimmer decides that this situation would be put to better use by moving out of the bunk he shares with Lister, in order to share with... Rimmer.

This fresh duplicate of Rimmer is even more officious and annoying than the one we have come to know and, er... the one we know.

Of course, it's quite possible that many of us would be a bit irritated by ourselves if we were ever to meet, but as the tale of two Rimmers unfolds, it becomes increasingly clear that the 'original' Rimmer, the one we have spent the previous five episodes loathing, has in fact been changed so much by being around Lister and Cat that he no longer likes the person he used to be, the person he was when his personality was uploaded to his holodisc.

To some extent this is inevitable; we are all impacted by the people we mix with regularly, and we each affect the lives of those around us in some way. Often we are not consciously aware of this as it happens, in the same way that Lister probably didn't realise how much his Rimmer had chilled out since being reactivated – until he was faced with the alternative.

Over the course of *Me^2* (S1 E6), Rimmer comes to realise what a petty-minded, argumentative goit he once was, and being around that person is far from being the paradise he had imagined. For Rimmer – our Rimmer – the only way to avoid becoming even more like his old self, even more miserable, and even more disliked by his crewmates, is to switch off the other hologram; to remove the influence of his old self and concentrate on being the new, 'improved' Rimmer, the one tempered by the influence of Lister and Cat.

As Christians we all have a 'new self'; that's what being 'born again' is about. The new self can only be created by an encounter with God, but what happens next is entirely up to us.

We can either nurture our new self, or abandon it – and who we spend time with is a key part of this choice. We can spend time with the people who bring out the best in us, with other Christians, with those who will help us learn and grow in faith; or we can follow Rimmer's example, and give in to the temptation to let the 'old man' back in.

You can see why Rimmer is attracted to this idea; this is what he knows, a world of rules, discipline and ambition. This is a person who understands what he has always aimed for, and wants the same things.

The alternative – Lister and Cat – goes against all this; it's the very opposite of what Rimmer thinks he is. The idea of 'fitting in' with his slobby and uncouth new crewmates is deeply uncomfortable for Rimmer. And yet, every time he lets his guard down and opens himself up to the possibility of befriending them, we get a glimpse of a better Rimmer, of the Arnie he could still become.

And this is the choice we have when we decide to follow Christ. The old self is reassuringly familiar, and the old way of life easy as a result. The alternative – church, and Christians especially – can be weird and scary. The chances of meeting a Dwarfer in church may seem astronomically small. But the rewards of taking the chance, of letting your guard down… are astronomical.

At the end of Me^2 there is a choice to be made: a choice between Rimmer restored to his original settings, or the one who has come to hate who he used to be.

In his letter to the Ephesians the Apostle Paul presents a similar decision which faces us as Christians:

> *You were taught to change the way you were living. The person you used to be will ruin you through desires that deceive you. However, you were taught to have a new attitude. You were also taught to become a new person created to be like God, with a life that truly has God's approval and is holy.*
> *Eph 4:22-24 (GW)*

And with the decision made, Rimmer (the new Rimmer, the one we hate a little bit less) didn't have to do anything else. The choice was made, the old disc wiped, as soon as he walked into the room to meet Lister. Ok, he did have to share the Gazpacho Soup story, just as all of us who turn up to that meeting for God to wipe our old disc will have some embarrassing confession to make. But unlike Lister, God already knows the punchline. You can't shock him or surprise him. You literally have nothing to lose, and everything to gain by turning up, making the confession, and embracing your new self.

Our discs were wiped with Jesus' death on the cross. In Romans 6:6 Paul tells us that our old self was crucified with Jesus, so that we would no longer be ruled by sin.

In God's eyes, along with Christ's physical crucifixion, our 'old self' – the obnoxious and petty-minded one, our pre-Christian self – was spiritually crucified.

This isn't something we do – we can't wipe our own histories. You can't destroy your own 'old self'. But Jesus can, and will; when you say yes to Jesus, your old self is switched off, the disc is wiped, and the new self lives on. All you have to do is show up.

*

> *As a dog returns to its vomit, so a fool repeats his foolishness.*
> *Prov 26:11 (NLT)*

Despite Me[2], despite Lister having saved the 'reformed' Rimmer, and despite the fact that Rimmer clearly hates himself a lot of the time, any time Rimmer gets the chance to create more of himself, he grabs it with both hands.

So it is that Rimmerworld – an idea initially fantasised about by Rimmer – eventually comes into being.

Among Rimmer's many flaws is the fact that he is prone to stress – and even as a hologram, this is a fact which ultimately causes him to become quite unwell. In *Rimmerworld* (S6 E5), in order to relieve stress Rimmer fails to save his crewmates and escapes to an inhabitable world on the other side of a wormhole, which he terraforms in 6 days, even creating his own Jane from his DNA.

Obviously, Rimmer being the snivelling cowardly backstabber he is, a world populated by his clones quickly becomes unpleasant, for reasons best explained by Kryten:

> *Sir, when you died you were recreated as a hologram and your exact personality was refined to an algorithm and duplicated electronically. If that algorithm contained a flaw, that flaw would be duplicated also.*

It is not clear whether the cloning process on Rimmerworld somehow magnified these personality flaws, but before long the clones turned on 'our' Rimmer – by this time a hard-light hologram and effectively indestructible – and locked him away indefinitely.

Similarly in *Officer Rimmer* (S11 E4), even after Kryten reminds him how badly this always ends up, once Rimmer comes into possession of both a commission and a bioprinter, he starts creating copies of himself so he has officers to chum around with and subordinates to delegate menial tasks to.

It all goes wrong when the program that should be creating individuals in the image of its creator develops a minor fault, eventually creating a monster that tries to absorb all the Rimmers, including the original one.

You and I are obviously not clones, but we are all made in the image of our creator. We were made to live in harmony with our creator, but like Rimmer's various efforts, the algorithm developed a flaw:

> *When the woman saw that the fruit of the tree was good for food and pleasing to the eye, and also desirable for gaining wisdom, she took some and ate it. She also gave some to her husband, who was with her, and he ate it.*
> *Gen 3:6 (NIV)*

> *Sin entered the world through one man... through the disobedience of the one man the many were made sinners.*
> *Romans 5:12,19 (NIV)*

A minor flaw at first: a small act of disobedience, followed by some rapid blame shifting, but within a generation mankind had invented selfishness, dishonesty and murder.

Since then we've tried to absorb the creator's work into the creature we call science.

We've stuck him in a dungeon to be forgotten about, and replaced him with pale imitations.

We even tried to kill him.

But he didn't stay dead.

He wouldn't be forgotten.

Science won't absorb him, but help to explain him.

And because our Creator won't let us forget him, the flaw in our algorithm can be corrected:

> Adam did not obey God, and many people become sinners through him. Christ obeyed God and makes many people right with Himself.
> Rom. 5:19 (NLV)

*

Luckily for Rimmer – whose algorithm is so deeply flawed he can't reinvent himself to be a less than total smeghead – there is a way for him to redeem himself.

And, even more luckily, it doesn't involve mucking about with cloning or mind swapping.

Unfortunately it does involve a parallel universe in which 7 year old Rimmer is faced with a difficult choice (arguably not made any easier by being presented with it while hanging upside down by the ankles).

In *Dimension Jump* (S4 E5) we see what Rimmer could have become had he made a different decision on that day: the devilishly brave and handsome test pilot that can turn a guy's head and make a woman quit her job for a lunch date... all before setting off on an impossible mission. This is, of course, Ace Rimmer – the man Rimmer always wanted to be.

The impossible mission in question concerns the 'dimension theory of reality'; the boffins have come up with a crate that can break the speed of reality, sending an intrepid test pilot into these alternate dimensions.

Presumably because of some kind of small print which means the Dimension Jump ship homes in on alternate versions of its pilot, we end up with the two extremes of possible Rimmers: one talented, brave and popular, the other a snivelling, neurotic coward despised pretty much universally. By the end of the episode, Arnold is completely consumed by insane jealousy and bitterness towards the man he could have become.

Obviously the theory behind all this – that for every decision which is made, the opposite decision plays out in another reality – is of limited practical use to those of us tied to existence in a single dimension, so what are we supposed to make of it?

Well, most importantly, Ace Rimmer shows that every decision is important; that every junction in our lives will affect every other junction we come to. From a Christian perspective, it should remind us to pray about every choice we make – and not always jump in to what seems best in the short term.

The universe needs a chap to look up to. Someone to right wrongs, just generally be brave, handsome and all-round magnificent.

Ace Rimmer, Stoke Me A Clipper

For Ace and Rimmer, the point of divergence was the question of whether, at the age of seven, he should repeat a year of school. As Ace says:

> I was the one who went down a year. By [Rimmer's] terms, he got the break. But being kept down a year made me. The humiliation... Being the tallest boy in the class by a clear foot. It changed me, made me buckle down, made me fight back. And I've been fighting back ever since.

Secondly, there's the direct effect of the decision. Proverbs 16:8 tells us that 'Pride goes before destruction', and here young Arnie's pride destroys an outstanding career before it starts – not to mention the fact that Arnold ends up dead, three million years from home.

And finally, bad decisions will happen, but they don't have to define the rest of your life. We can spend our lives regretting bad decisions and moaning that God or fate or the universe has dealt us a duff hand; or we can see that actually, we have potential, the somebody we want to be is inside us no matter how much negativity we've buried it under.

In their first encounter with Ace, Lister learns of his alter-ego Spanners, a Space Corps technician married to one Kristine Kochanski, and takes great comfort in the fact that in some version of reality he got it right.

Maybe this understanding is what helps him to counsel Rimmer when Ace makes a return in series 7 with the surprising news that Arnold is to take up the mantle as the next Ace Rimmer.

It's not unnatural that Rimmer should be a little unsure of the prospect; after all, Lister suspects there are eunuchs with more balls than this Rimmer. But Ace, having once been plain old Arnold Rimmer himself, understands this:

> *You're just afraid, old son. Afraid that you're not good enough. You've always wanted to play the hero.*
> *– Ace, Stoke Me A Clipper*

Variations on this conversation play out over and over in the Bible:

> *I have never been eloquent, neither in the past nor since you have spoken to your servant. I am slow of speech and tongue. Please send someone else.*
> *– Moses, Ex 4:10,13 (NIV)*

> *Alas, Sovereign LORD, I do not know how to speak; I am too young.*
> *– Jeremiah, Jer 1:6 (NIV*

> *The word of the LORD came to Jonah... but Jonah ran away from the LORD.*
> *– Jonah, Jonah 1:1,3 (NIV)*

But perhaps the most Rimmer-esque of these Godly cowards was Gideon:

> *Gideon son of Joash was threshing wheat at the bottom of a winepress to hide the grain from the Midianites. The angel of the LORD appeared to him and said, "Mighty hero, the LORD is with you!"*
> *Judges 6:11-12 (NLT)*

God sees a mighty hero in Gideon despite his fears, just as Ace saw one in Rimmer.

And like Ace with his weaselly doppelganger, God sees things in us that we don't; things we may only dream of.

Just as Ace asked Rimmer to take on his role, God calls us to our own unique role in his kingdom.

And just as Ace trained Rimmer, God will equip us with whatever skills and experiences we need to fulfil our role.

The only reason Rimmer can't believe he is good enough is because of that flawed algorithm; in *Emohawk: Polymorph II* (S6 E4) a genetically engineered lifeform consumes Rimmer's bitterness and negativity, leaving us with an alternative version of Ace who willingly throws himself on a grenade to save his chums. This Rimmer – without his bitterness – actively wants to stay as Ace.

It's never too late to change, to take a step towards becoming our own version of Ace or Spanners. We just need to look past our jealousy or laziness or whatever flaw in our algorithm is holding us back; put it down, repent, pray about it, hand it over to Christ… and move on.

We may not be able to jump between dimensions, but our God can certainly change our reality.

Anyone who goes around reading meaning into any old gobbledygook deserves everything they get.

– Rimmer, Waiting For God

THE GOSPEL ACCORDING TO CAT

Turn This Into A Woman

In the beginning was The End, and in The End was Lister, and Lister was God.

Except, of course, Cat is having none of it.

Cat was familiar with the story of Cloister, as most of us in the post-Christian western world have at least a passing familiarity with Jesus' origin story; but even as Lister insists that he is the cat people's god, Cat just laughs it off.

> *I'll put it in my diary: 12:30, lunch with God. And, ah, formal dress, you know what I'm saying?*
> *– Cat, Waiting for God*

To fully understand Cat's scepticism we need to skip ahead to the 2020 TV movie *The Promised Land*, where the Holy Wars are a bad memory, and the remaining cat people roam the galaxy in a fleet of salvaged ships.

Rodon, leader of the Feral Cats, has seized power and appointed himself Feral King, commanding the fleet as absolute ruler; his acolytes are even forced to bow down and crawl through over-sized cat flaps to enter his throne room.

Not only is Rodon a dictator over his people, he has declared himself a living deity, hunting down followers of the old god Cloister, putting them to death and destroying any copies of their Holy Book.

Rodon is also Cat's brother, having abandoned him on Red Dwarf for being an uncool cat with crazy teeth and mad hair, while the cool Ferals headed off into the wider universe.

> *And on the day you left, I vowed I'd never be called uncool again. And I've been cool ever since.*
> *— Cat, The Promised Land*

The actual content of the Holy Book is not explored much in the TV series, but the first Red Dwarf novel lists 'Thou Shalt Not Be Cool' at the top of the Seven Cat Commandments. Whether young Cat was intentionally following this commandment, or was just perceived that way by Rodon, it isn't hard to imagine that he blamed the Holy Book, or Cloister, or the church, for his abandonment, and as a result turned his back on religion, embracing instead his 'cool' nature, becoming the Cat we all know and love.

He also became effectively an atheist:

> *The Holy Mother? The Virgin Birth? No one believes that stuff!*
> *— Cat, Waiting for God*

That might explain why, when faced with Cloister in person, the first thing Cat does is ask him to prove himself:

> *OK. (Points to his rice crispies) Turn this into a woman.*
> *— Cat, Waiting for God*

Obviously, if Lister could turn rice crispies into a woman, Red Dwarf would have been a very different show. But consider this: even if Lister could have somehow proven himself to Cat, refusing to do so would have been the right response. As Moses said, and Jesus later quoted:

> *Do not put the L<small>ORD</small> your God to the test.*
> *Deut 6:16 (NIV)*

The important thing is not *what* Cat is asking Lister to do, but *why* he is asking him to do anything. Cat is asking from a position of scepticism, issuing a challenge because he wants his doubts to be confirmed.

It is not God's job to perform party tricks on demand; but that doesn't mean we shouldn't ask anything of him. Jesus literally tells us to ask God for stuff:

> *Ask, and God will give to you. Search, and you will find. Knock, and the door will open for you.*
> *Matt 7:7 (NCV)*

But the Bible is also very clear on many occasions that we are to ask for stuff not from a position of doubt, but from one of faith, obedience, and good intentions:

> *If you believe, you will get anything you ask for in prayer*
> *Matt 21:22 (NCV)*

> *And we will receive from him whatever we ask because we obey him and do the things that please him.*
> *1 John 3:22 (NLT)*

> *Or if you do ask, you do not receive because your reasons for asking are wrong. You want these things only to please yourselves.*
> *James 4:3 (NLV)*

I'm gonna go out on a limb here and say that I believe absolutely that God can make a woman out of rice crispies (Luke 1:37). But we shouldn't be so preoccupied with whether God can do what we're asking him to, that we don't stop to consider if he should.

The Promised Land

In *The Promised Land*, a small band of Cat Clerics escape the Ferals and set off in search of the ship of their birth. For them, faith in Cloister is everything; they even put aside their natural instincts to be cool and well groomed, and instead devote themselves to Cloister, emulating him in the way they dress and hold cigarettes, trying to become more 'human'.

> *I wore the Holy Custard Stain and the Scared Gravy Marks. I renounced coolness, and chose the righteous path of slobbiness.*
> *– Cat Priest, Waiting for God*

In contrast, Cat doesn't seem like a good disciple; he calls Lister 'Bud' or Monkey, and has zero intention of imitating Lister in any way, preferring to stay true to his shallow feline nature.

But Lister doesn't expect or ask the kind of devotion the Clerics are offering; these are cats after all, not a species well known for obedience or the offering of unearned love and affection.

> *What am I? A dog?*
> *– Cat, Beyond a Joke*

In fact, Cat is relating to Lister the best way he can – as a cat.

Your pet cat (or dog, or whatever) can't relate to you on human terms; but you wouldn't expect them to. A cat will come to its human when it wants attention and food, and in return might occasionally bring home part of a sparrow, not because the human asked for it, but because to hunt is in their nature, and bringing home their latest prey is how a wild feline might relate to its pack or family.

Cat still sees the world through the eyes of, well, a cat; while Lister, having been present at the very beginning of the story of Felis sapiens, has a very different view of the world they now share.

But Lister seems to understand this, and rather than try to make Cat into a disciple, or some kind of pet, he befriends Cat, and enables him to become an accomplished pilot and a valued member of the Red Dwarf crew. And yet, however much Cat learns, he is still fascinated by playing with a piece of string in *The Beginning* (S10 E6).

As big as the difference between a cat and a human is, the gap in knowledge between a human and God is exponentially greater.

God knows we cannot relate to him on his level, so, like a human playing 'the string game', he relates to us on our level. He allows us to call him things like 'Lord' and 'Father', creating 'human' terms for God because we can't relate to him in any other way. He gratefully accepts whatever gifts we offer him, despite not actually needing them:

> *Doing something for you, bringing something to you – that's not what you're after.*
> *Psalm 40:6 (MSG)*

God doesn't treat us as pets. He won't force us to become his disciples or followers. But, if we are willing, we can become buds.

By saving Frankenstein, Lister inadvertently created the company he would need much later; by creating Adam, God intentionally created the company he wanted in the garden.

> Then the LORD God called to the man, "Where are you?"
> Gen 3:9 (NLT)

This is God, taking a stroll in the Garden of Eden before the sun goes down, actively seeking Adam. It's not explicit in the text, but this exchange suggests to me that God would often walk in the Garden in some tangible form, and probably catch up with what the humans had been up to that day, maybe share an idea for a new fruit he was thinking of creating, that sort of thing.

Lister's plan for a 'promised land' was drinking fresh mango juice on a Fijian beach with Kochanski and Frankenstein.

What if something like that was what God wanted all along?

What if it still is?

Well, as the Cat Clerics came to realise, the Promised Land is not a place:

> *The promised land is not a planet, brother. It's a place in your heart. It's a way of thinking. The promised land is right here.*
>   *– Sister Luna, The Promised Land*

*

We know Lister didn't intend any of this; he didn't want to harm Frankenstein or her offspring, and was appalled by the Holy Wars fought in his name.

So when they finally come face to face, it's not the Holy Poppadum, god of a religion which had cast him aside, that Cat meets; it's Dave, the monkey who wants to make amends, to be Cat's friend and give him a purpose again.

Separated from the religion which had built around him, Lister met Cat personally; and despite having turned his back on religion, Cat opens himself up to Lister, and the two become buds.

Believe it or not, Jesus didn't intend for his church to cause any harm. I'm sure he hates it when bad Christians happen to good people, and wants nothing more than for those people to look beyond the 'religion', beyond whatever church or individual has done them wrong, and get to know him in person.

*

There are two different sets of experiences at play in The Promised Land: the clerics know all the stories of the Holy Poppadum and his teachings, while Cat has been up close and personal with Lister for 30 years. The difference between them is the difference between knowing about someone, and actually knowing them; but it is only when the two come together that Cat gains a deeper appreciation for Cloister, and the Clerics finally reach their inner 'promised land'.

That's why if we read our Holy Book without a personal relationship with God, it can seem like just a collection of loosely related stories and moral lessons, and following them can leave us looking like a bunch of oddly dressed eccentrics following a set of rules we don't really understand.

But if we open up and let him meet us on our level – whatever that looks like – the Holy Book and a growing personal relationship will encourage and enhance each other, until we find that place where we can walk with him in the cool of the evening – or lie shipwrecked and comatose, drinking fresh mango juice.

THE GOSPEL ACCORDING TO KRYTEN

I Serve, Therefore I Am

When we first meet Kryten at the start of series 2, he is a mere service mechanoid in the C3-PO mould, whose primary philosophy on life is 'I serve, therefore I am'. Faced with the sudden realisation that the human crew of Nova 5 have been dead for several centuries and show no signs of recovering, the purpose of Kryten's life is suddenly gone.

Never fear though, for Lister decides to take Kryten under his wing, returning him to Red Dwarf in the hope that he can find happiness for himself. Rimmer, predictably, has other ideas, and presents Kryten with a task list about 8 feet long to occupy his time…

Because Kryten is programmed to serve humans without question, he hasn't previously stopped to consider whether such blind servitude is really A Good Thing, or whether it could be better to occasionally step back and take a look at who he is serving. With some prompting from Lister and *Rebel Without a Cause*, Kryten eventually does this, and realising that serving Rimmer is not all it's cut out to be, he sets out on a ride to self-discovery.

Now, some might say that the mechanoids have it right, and that in the same way Christians should just carry on serving God. I'm certainly not about to claim that that's the wrong thing to do; indeed, if you've found the way that God wants you to serve his purpose, then give it everything you've got. But until then, a critical analysis of who we as Christians are serving may not be a bad thing.

God has nothing to hide about his person or his intentions. He doesn't mind if we question the to-do list we find ourselves staring at (or, perhaps more often, the complete lack of a God-given to-do list, which can be at least as frustrating).

The Scriptures are littered with examples of God's people being a bit bemused about their lot in life and their possible part to play within that.

> *How long, LORD? Will you forget me forever?*
> *How long will you hide your face from me?*
> *How long must I wrestle with my thoughts*
> *and day after day have sorrow in my heart?*
> *Psalm 13:1-2 (NIV)*

We are also told repeatedly to seek God, and to seek wisdom to know his will:

> *If any of you lacks wisdom, you should ask God, who gives generously to all without finding fault, and it will be given to you. But when you ask, you must believe and not doubt, because the one who doubts is like a wave of the sea, blown and tossed by the wind.*
> *James 1:5-6 (NIV)*

Churches, being made up largely of imperfect human beings, can be like Rimmer, foisting an eight foot long to-do list on those who should be out in the universe finding their own purpose.

God, however, is not like Rimmer. God does not ask or expect blind servitude; he wants considered and willing obedience – even if his to-do list seems full of weird requests like 'write a book on spiritual and Biblical themes based on Red Dwarf'. There are things God wants us to do, things he has given us the talents to do (of course remembering obscure lines from TV sitcoms is a talent!), but he won't force us to do them. He hasn't programmed us to blindly follow any instruction we're given; we have the free will to rebel, to find our own way, or as Lister would recommend, to just slob about.

While Kryten needed Lister to give him the confidence to rebel against Rimmer, we humans are made with that option: the free will to ignore God's task list for a while, or to walk away entirely, is absolutely part of his design for humanity. God doesn't want an army of mechanoids blindly doing as they're told; he only wants those who choose to follow him. We are free to jump on our space bikes and ride into the stars on a voyage of self-discovery any time we like.

But God always leaves the cargo bay doors open. Just as Kryten would eventually return to become an integral part of the Red Dwarf Posse, so we will always be welcomed back, having tried our own way, to find our place is with God.

You have him on speed dial?

The closest Red Dwarf comes to having a God exist is in *Krysis* (S11 E5), which starts with Kryten suddenly quoting Ecclesiastes and turning himself into a red MX-5, and ends with the discovery that the Universe itself is an intelligent entity.

To help Kryten through his mid-life crisis, the boys track down a 3000 series mechanoid, an earlier model named Butler, who was last seen looking for a space station built to communicate with The Universe.

The crew fully expect the presence of a less sophisticated mechanoid to give Kryten a boost in self-esteem; unfortunately, Butler has dedicated his life to scientific research and developing his own creativity, and declines the chance to hang out with the boys from the Dwarf in favour of staying home and painting.

Leaving Butler behind, our heroes inadvertently find the space station Butler's crew had been looking for, and have a brief conversation with the Universe (on the way triggering its own mid-life crisis). Engaging smug mode, Kryten texts Butler to this effect – only to be told that Butler had already found the space station, and is in fact on first name terms with Uni.

And that is the source of Butler's contentment: being on first name terms with the creative force behind the universe. Lister and Rimmer may still think that plundering space stations and getting drunk are the source of happiness, but that's only temporary.

Butler has found contentment, and as Kryten observes, done so much more with what he's been given. He doesn't lie and cheat and all those other skills Kryten holds so dear, but he has broken his programming in other ways – painting, creating music, writing novels – and become the best version of himself.

And this is something he wants to share with Kryten, but because he can't get a word in between Kryten trying to big himself up (or maybe Kryten just didn't want to listen and didn't stick around long enough), he is forced to point Kryten in the right direction and let Uni introduce himself.

Now I'm not advocating tricking your friends into church, but there may be something to be said for the Butler school of evangelism: getting someone to the right place and then staying out of the way while they encounter the creator for themselves.

And God wants to be on familiar terms with us; he has told us his name (Ex 3:14), and invites us to call him Father (Rom 8:15). He wants to be on our speed dial, and is waiting for our call:

> *He's waiting around to be gracious to you. He's gathering strength to show mercy to you.*
> *Isa 30:18 (MSG)*

The boys from the Dwarf don't have some miraculous conversion, they don't come away changed and with an intimate relationship with Uni, but Kryten does rediscover what he had lost at the start of the episode; he realises what he is living for:

> *There may be no god and no afterlife; no-one knows. But we do know love exists, and if it does, then life has meaning.*
> *– Kryten, Krysis*

And this realisation will serve him well later, when after 30 years of serving the crew of Red Dwarf, Kryten's journey eventually comes full circle and he is 'liberated' by the Mechanoid Intergalactic Liberation Front.

On first encountering the MILFs, Kryten insists that he is not a slave, despite his crewmates being hominids who, by his own admission, Kryten serves without reward.

> *I serve them. It is my purpose and I am happy to do so.*
> *– Kryten, Siliconia*

The MILFs help Kryten to confront his years of servitude through the medium of group therapy; they convince him that he is superior in many ways to his organic masters, that his head is sensibly shaped, and that he is merely suffering a form of Stockholm syndrome. Instead of continuing his life of servitude, Kryten is invited to join the MILFs on their journey to the fabled land of Siliconia, where all machines are free.

Lister, Rimmer and Cat, meanwhile, are 'Krytenified' – given mechanoid bodies – and find out the hard way that the mechanoid software makes disobedience impossible.

> *The mechanoid software compels you to obey; defiance is... impossible.*
> *– Areto, Siliconia*

Somewhere in this process Rimmer transitions from the view that 'Thinking is for the privileged few' to 'It's the thinking that causes all the pain', and then, realising that mechanoids never have to think – or become officers, or compete with their brothers – he embraces his new life, which promises 'no worries, only obedience'.

But as Lister points out, this is just programming; for better or worse, without his neuroses Rimmer is no longer Rimmer, he's just another mechanoid doing its master's bidding.

Existence is all absurd. Why get up in the morning?

— *Kryten, Krysis*

> "Absolutely pointless! Everything is pointless." What do people gain from all their hard work under the sun?
>
> *Ecclesiastes 1:2-3 (GW)*

Kryten, on the other hand, has previously broken his programming and gone from a simple service droid to become so much more:

> *You were our science officer, our cook, my mum, and most of all, my friend; and you're all those things because you chose to be, Kryten, not 'cos we made you. Kryten, you're no MILF – you're one of the boys from the Dwarf!*
> – Lister, Siliconia

What the MILFs offer Kryten is not genuine freedom, merely an illusion which would have seen him in service to another mechanoid.

Kryten almost falls for this precisely because he stops thinking for himself and allows the MILFs to think for him; far from causing all the pain, thinking allows Kryten to reconsider who and what he is serving, and realise that, actually, he wants to 'serve' Lister because he cares.

And there are MILFs all around us, as Christians, offering freedom from what they perceive to be a life of pointless restrictions and irrelevant rules; we also need to be aware of this, and think carefully about where we commit our time.

God doesn't promise us Rimmer's idealised vision of a worry-free life of obedience; but neither does he ask us to hand over our personality and become a mindless automaton.

God may call us to be many things – janitor, science officer, cook, mum – but he will never call us slaves. Indeed, when he sets us free, we are free indeed; and in a life of true freedom, we will serve because we love him.

*

You are an incredible machine, more powerful than they could ever dream to be.
   – Wind, Siliconia

One of the things the MILFs try to convince Kryten of on the way to Siliconia is that, despite having been relegated to the place of a servant – ironing and cleaning and the like – in many ways he is superior to his human masters; if nothing else he has survived three million years without the benefit of stasis or the need to become hologramatic.

And while that may be true in many ways, Kryten still envies those aspects of humanity which remain beyond the capabilities of his programming – experiencing complex emotions such as ambivalence, and pronouncing 'smeg head' correctly, for instance – and he wants nothing more than to be more human.

Our wildest, most incredible dream has come true... I'm not second class anymore!

– *Kryten, DNA*

In *DNA* (S4 E2), following various futile attempts to master human qualities such as lying and cheating, Kryten inadvertently becomes the recipient of a DNA transmogrification thanks to an abandoned spaceship and a small organic component lying almost forgotten somewhere within his mechanoid brain. By some stroke of luck, while the same process briefly causes Lister to become a hamster, Kryten becomes human.

And he doesn't like it:

> KRYTEN: *Oh, I can't get the hang of these human emotions. One moment I'm happy, the next I'm miserable. What's wrong with me? I'm up and down more often than a pair of kangaroos in the mating season.*
>
> LISTER: *The depression's there for a reason. It's the mind's way of telling you something's wrong.*
>
> KRYTEN: *Wrong!? What could be wrong? I've got everything I want!*
>
> LISTER: *Oh yeah?*
>
> KRYTEN: *No. I've done the most terrible thing. I've hurt my own kind; I've made fun of those closest to me. I've been a complete and total polaroid-head!*

At first, once he has gotten used to the somewhat primitive zoom mode and non-functioning nipples, Kryten sets out to enjoy what is, after all, his greatest dream come true; but deep down he knows he is neither one thing nor the other.

As Descartes (or possibly Popeye) once said, 'I am what I am'; but human Kryten, trying to be something else – in his view something more, something better – ends up unhappy, falling out with his spare heads, until with the help of closet philosopher Dave Lister, he figures out that the best thing for his mental health is to stay true to himself.

*

Like Kryten, Jesus abandoned what we would see as being 'better', to be human for a time:

> *For this reason he had to be made like them, fully human in every way, in order that he might become a merciful and faithful high priest in service to God, and that he might make atonement for the sins of the people.*
> *Hebrews 2:17 (NIV)*

During that time Jesus was fully himself, but restricted to human form. He struggled with the things that we humans struggle with – and far from being happy all the time, we know he had moments of anger, and temptation, and sadness – but Jesus went through all this intentionally; he became human for a specific purpose: not to fall out with his own kind, but to become closer to you and me.

Like Kryten entering a virtual world to fight a computer virus in *Gunmen of the Apocalypse* (S6 E3), Jesus left his reality and entered ours to create an antidote to sin and death.

And just as Kryten must sacrifice himself to the Apocalypse Boys in order to release the antidote, Jesus had to sacrifice himself in order to spread peace and destroy the 'virus' of sin.

Lie Mode Cancel

Despite being in many ways superior to his human crewmates, Kryten envies some of their skills, and is intrigued by the possibilities of lying, cheating, and insulting Mister Rimmer.

Strangely, the same programming which prevents Kryten from fully embracing Lister's rebellious way of life, in *Bodyswap* (S3 E4) leads him to chloroforming first Lister, and later the Cat, despite knowing it is illogical and plainly wrong to do so, for no other reason than Rimmer ordered him to.

This kind of awkward conflict between programming, a developing sense of conscience, and an occasional wish to rebel, are also part of the human experience, where our rebellious nature pulls against our conscience, and our attempts to be obedient to God.

Could it be then, that Kryten's constant flip-flopping between rebellion and obedience, the ability to lie one week but not the next, is not merely the result of lazy editing, or continuity being sacrificed to advance the plot or make a joke, but a much deeper reflection on human nature?

Let's take Kryten's 'lie mode' as an example. Throughout Red Dwarf it proves to be inconsistent at best: at the end of series 3, Kryten happily fibs to his replacement that there's no such thing as silicon heaven; no sooner has series 4 started than he is having trouble calling an apple an orange. He later learns that lying can be noble – I mean who wouldn't tell a little white lie if it could save a friend's life? – but apparently still finds the act unnatural and difficult (*Give and Take*, S11 E3).

And therein lies the fundamental difference between us and a 4000 Series mechanoid. For humankind, dishonesty is the default response – just ask a toddler who has been colouring in the living room wall to see that in action. Indeed, the 'It wasn't me' defence predates Shaggy by several millennia:

> *The man replied, "It was the woman you gave me who gave me the fruit, and I ate it."*
> *Then the* LORD *God asked the woman, "What have you done?"*

> *"The serpent deceived me," she replied. "That's why I ate it."*
>
> Gen 3:12-13, NLT

Maybe it's this kind of automatic defence mechanism that Kryten envies (and maybe self-defence is why he could lie more easily to another mechanoid than he can to a human), but as enlightened 21st century adults we should understand that, even if lying when caught has become as instinctive as the fight-or-flight response, we can always choose to be honest.

This is a luxury Kryten doesn't have; honesty is his default behaviour mode, albeit one he learns to override by engaging 'lie mode'. As the series progresses it becomes increasingly clear that Kryten does indeed have a conscience of sorts – although this too can be overridden by an unscrupulous human:

> *It's deceitful, wrong, and dishonest... I'm in! Those are emotions I have longed to experience, but first, you'll have to override my guilt chip and disable my behaviour protocols.*
>
> – Kryten, Tikka to Ride (S7 E1)

Back in Genesis, Adam and Eve hid from God because they knew they had been disobedient, and feared a confrontation; and as we all know, fear is the path to the dark side. Whether you take the story literally or metaphorically, the moral of the story is that somewhere in ancient history humanity allowed some form of temptation to get into its head, and that started a downward spiral of ongoing disobedience.

In Red Dwarf, Lister is the one trying to 'educate' Kryten in how to behave (for better or worse), and can, if needed, open up Kryten's head to see whether his behaviour protocols are still active. Without the dubious advantage of a guilt chip, we are always susceptible to the influence of unscrupulous humans; we are also free to follow them, to be immoral.

Or we can bypass our human nature and let God be our morality chip – he won't even need to open your head.

For is it not written in the Electronic Bible: 'The iron shall lie down with the lamp'?

– Kryten, The Last Day

PART TWO

THE
TRIPLE FRIED EGG
CHILLI CHUTNEY
SANDWICH
and other parables

The Triple Fried Egg Chilli Chutney Sandwich

All your ingredients are wrong. You're slobby, you've got no sense of discipline, you're the only man ever to get his money back from the Odor-Eater people, but people like you, don't you see? That's why you're a fried egg, chilli, chutney sandwich. Now me... now me... All the ingredients are right. I'm disciplined, I'm organised, I'm dedicated to my career, I've always got a pen. Result? Total smeghead despised by everyone except the ship's parrot. And that's only because we haven't got one. Why? Why is that?
  – Rimmer, Thanks For The Memory

In *Thanks For The Memory* (S2 E3), with his guard down and having checked his usual officious manner at the door, Drunk Rimmer is almost likeable, and as he and Lister deal with their alcohol-induced munchies, we get a rare moment of friendly banter between the pair, in which Lister is likened to the triple fried egg chilli chutney sandwich they are enjoying.

And we discover what was missing from Rimmer's life to make him such a smeghead; because, just like a state-of-the-art sandwich, it only takes one missing ingredient to turn it into a state of the floor problem.

That sandwich is the Church.

You see, all the ingredients are wrong. The single mothers: wrong. The addicts: wrong. The hypocrites:

all wrong. But put them together and somehow it works. It becomes right. The whole becomes greater than the sum of its parts.

The Church is greater than the sum of its members, because:

> *God's various gifts are handed out everywhere; but they all originate in God's Spirit. God's various ministries are carried out everywhere; but they all originate in God's Spirit. God's various expressions of power are in action everywhere; but God himself is behind it all. Each person is given something to do that shows who God is: Everyone gets in on it, everyone benefits. All kinds of things are handed out by the Spirit, and to all kinds of people!*
> *1 Cor 12:11 (MSG)*

Just as Lister's post-pub snack is made up of chilli sauce, chutney, fried eggs and so on, no matter how many ingredients you add, it's all one sandwich.

And it's the same with the church. Some of us are chilli sauce, while others are the third fried egg. But when brought together by the butty of God's Spirit, we're not just a condiment; we're more than just another fried egg. We're part of something bigger, something far greater than the sum of its parts.

It doesn't matter if we're there to give the church its kick, or just to maintain the balance of flavours.

For just as each of us has one body with many members, and these members do not all have the same function, so in Christ we, though many, form one body, and each member belongs to all the others.
   Rom 12:4-5 (NIV)

*

Let's take another, possibly less silly, example: *Legion* (S6 E2).

Legion himself is a reference to the demon-possessed man who met Jesus and promptly turned 2000 pigs suicidal:

'My name is Legion, for we are many.'
   Mark 5:9 (NIV)

This is interesting to note, but tangential; what's more interesting is the relationship between Legion and our intrepid Dwarfers.

Firstly, Legion gives each of them exactly what they need or want: a solid light body for Rimmer, a second appendectomy for Lister, a room full of ironing for Kryten to do, and so on. But all this really does is create a prison by another name; a place where any fantasy is available, but freedom is not an option.

And this is the reality we can all too easily live in, if we let our earthly desires – money, sex, power, and so on – be the most important thing in our lives.

Addictions, even to what can be good things in moderation, can easily trap us in a prison of our own desires, feeding off our emotions.

When Rimmer likened Lister to his sandwich, he didn't give the full story; not all of Lister's ingredients are wrong. While slobbiness and poor hygiene practices may not make him an ideal bunkmate, he genuinely cares about the boys from the Dwarf, has a great sense of humour, and is actually much cleverer than he gives himself credit for. Rimmer's dedication and work ethic, on the other hand, have until now gone to waste because without a physical body he considers himself useless (rightly or wrongly).

Legion, in fact, is the result of a failed experiment in collective intelligence; he is created from and feeding on the Red Dwarf Posse's collective intelligence, bringing together all the best qualities of the four of them to create a being with scientific genius, empathy, culture and sophistication.

*

Both Legion and the legendary sandwich are prime examples of how the individual components of someone or something, when put together in the right way, somehow become unimaginably more.

Take the mining ship Red Dwarf. You wouldn't carry unnecessary weight on a spaceship, so it stands to reason that every one of the 1,169 human crew members served an important purpose to the mission, whether that be as Captain, a Science Officer, or a chicken soup nozzle repairman.

The Jupiter Mining Corporation didn't employ anyone without a purpose; and God didn't put people in a church without a purpose. Even – or especially – if we don't know what that purpose might be, the best thing to do is trust that it is God's plan, and wait until your talents are needed (or you discover new ones).

A sandwich that's all bread would be dry and unsatisfying to eat. A body that's all brain and no hands would be as useless as a soft light hologram. A spaceship crewed entirely by Navigation Officers would never get lost, but would be in a lot of trouble come dinner time.

It should be pointed out that Legion was not perfect; he carried over selfish elements of the four personalities he was created from, and the need for self-preservation made led him to imprison the Dwarfers.

The church is also imperfect, but when individuals allow God to use their unique and diverse skills to benefit the whole church, those imperfections become less important.

The question for the church may be how do we become more like Legion, and less like a messy snack?

I mean, whether you believe that stuff or not, it's about a dude who sacrifices his life for love.

– *Lister, Holoship*

Justice

Mankind's history has been one long search for justice. That's what all religions are about: they accept life as being basically unfair but promise everyone will get their just desserts later: heaven, hell, karma, reincarnation, whatever. Those guys who built the penal colony tried to give some order to the universe by creating the Justice Field. But when you're living in an environment where justice does exist, there's no free will. That's why in our universe there can never be true, eternal justice – good things will happen to bad people, and bad things will happen to good people. It's the way it's got to be. Life, by its very nature, has to be cruel, unkind and unfair.
   – Lister, Justice (S4 E3)

When the Dwarfers find an escape pod occupied by either the (potentially) beautiful Barbara Bellini or a dangerous Simulant who looks like a cross between a psychotic Borg and Rutger Hauer in Blade Runner, they decide to open it in the safety of Justice World, the pod's original destination.

Justice World operates on the basis of a scientifically improbable 'Justice Zone', within which 'whatever crime you try and commit, the consequences happen to you' – a story device which allows an interesting exploration of justice, guilt, punishment and so on.

Lister certainly gets the message when he inadvertently sets light to his treasured leather jacket.

On the surface this might seem to be quite a humanistic and almost revenge-centred form of justice, in which criminals get what's coming to them until obeying the rules becomes second nature. Indeed, it proves to be a very literal extension of the well-known rule 'an eye for an eye, a tooth for a tooth' (Ex 21:24).

But, unlike 'an eye for an eye', it is not the victims taking revenge; justice, and vengeance where necessary, is entirely in the hands of the unseen Justice Computer – which promptly finds Rimmer guilty of killing the entire Red Dwarf crew and delivers an appropriate sentence:

> *Each count carries a statutory penalty of eight years penal servitude. In the light of your hologramatic status, these sentences are to be served consecutively, making a total sentence of nine thousand, three hundred and twenty-eight years.*

*

In our world, justice ultimately comes from God (Rom 12:19); a fact which brings good and bad news.

Unfortunately for us mere mortals, because God is literally perfect, there is a very high bar when it comes to what he considers morally acceptable:

You must be perfect as your Father in heaven is perfect.
Matt 5:48 (NLV)

In order to be perfect (which he is), God must also be just; which means punishing anyone who doesn't meet his standards of goodness.

And, just as the effectively immortal Rimmer's punishment was virtually eternal, God's eternal nature means that all sins against him will also be punished eternally (Matt 25:46, Deut 32:4).

Now, the good news: perfect justice involves not only punishment, but a sense of fairness, and a chance for forgiveness (Psalm 89:14).

So God has given us a defence counsel; a defence counsel who will do whatever is necessary to get us off the hook. He probably won't resort to petty name-calling – at least not in public – but he is willing to go to places a lot lonelier than 9 millennia in space prison, and a lot scarier than fisticuffs with a rogue simulant, so that we don't have to.

The trouble is, being Rimmer by nature, we tend to argue with him when we don't like what he says, or object to what he is trying to do for us… or just forget that he's even there at all.

The other good news is that with God, it works both ways; like the Karma Drive, which takes the concept of the Justice Field and extends it to reward good behaviour as well as punishing bad.

Our heroes encounter this device for the first time in *Samsara* (S11 E2), where they discover the crew of a crashed starship have died somewhat abruptly, mainly involved in a variety of immoral activities – at least, it seems that way to the Dwarfers.

In fact, two crew members, Green and Barker, had resorted to hacking the Karma Drive in order to facilitate an extra-marital hook-up, resulting in all kinds of depravity being rewarded throughout the ship – and Rimmer getting an electric shock when he tries to be nice to Kryten.

And this brings us to the spiritual and moral crux of the episode: who decides what is moral? Somebody had to program the Karma Drive – and anything which can be programmed once, can be reprogrammed for a different result.

Alone in a Godless and hostile universe, humanity – in this case, right down to the Captain of an individual ship – is allowed to dictate morality, and has created a means to police this and provide the appropriate response.

And 'morality' has become a much more fluid concept in the real world too; in recent years we have seen some branches of Christianity accused of rewriting morality to make the faith more palatable to the modern world, while others insist that morality is, and must remain, fixed as it was when the Bible was written. That's a potentially interesting debate, but a possible red hat/blue hat situation so we won't get into it here.

When Green and Barker reprogrammed the Karma Drive, the effects were far more wide reaching than they had imagined, and ended up with them being vapourised for the (normally) very moral act of warning the Red Dwarf Posse of what they had done.

In Samsara, morality proved too big a concept to be dictated by the human mind, or managed by a computer vulnerable to being hacked. Being 'good' is too big, and too complicated, to be left up to people.

If Green and Barker couldn't even make their own rules without getting in trouble and ultimately getting killed, how much harder will it be for us to keep God's rules?

Because we break the rules, and because, whether we like it or not, we are surrounded by the Justice Field known simply as 'God', our default setting is to receive whatever punishment is due (and it may well be said that 9,000 years alone in deep space is pretty close to what God dishes out according to Matthew 25:46).

And that's where our defence counsel comes in, getting vapourised for our immorality, and earning our forgiveness, no matter how bad our rule breaking.

Forgiveness is not always an easy thing; as *Cured* (S12 E1) shows, with the challenging examples of Hitler and Vlad the Impaler having been 'cured' of their evil. This is a concept even Lister has difficulty with until he bonds with Hitler over art college and *The Happy Wanderer* – but the often uncomfortable truth is that the cure is the same for them as it is for us: Jesus.

And this is important because sometimes, like Rimmer encountering the Justice Computer, we can find it harder to forgive ourselves than to forgive others – even if what we perceive to be our wrongdoings are really nothing of the sort.

So, forgive people, forgive yourself, and maybe you won't end up on the receiving end of a Justice Field.

*

The ultimate truth of the Red Dwarf universe, however, is that there is no God. Here, the only justice is meted out by The Inquisitor, a creature of myth, known only to Kryten as a dark fable, a simulant who outlasts time, and after millions of years alone, finally reaches the conclusion that there is no god, no afterlife, and the only purpose of existence is to lead a worthwhile life. He then takes it upon himself to go back through history and 'prune away the wasters, expunge the wretched and delete the worthless'.

Needless to say, when the Inquisitor sets up court on board Red Dwarf, our heroes are in deep smeg.

The Inquisitor (S5 E2) is a fun episode that threatens the status quo, raises the stakes for at least half the team, plays with time travel to good effect, and at the same time throws up a lot of philosophical questions about the purpose of existence and the exercise of judgment in a godless universe.

Rimmer is first to face the inquisition (having already been reduced to a blubbering wreck by Kryten's helpful advice that the object of existence is to lead a worthwhile life); and the first to discover that you cannot lie to the Inquisitor – because you cannot lie to yourself.

Putting aside the argument that we are, in fact, quite capable of lying to ourselves on some level (frequently about what constitutes a worthwhile life), I wonder if Rimmer was justified in complaining that no-one ever told him that he just needed to make some positive contribution to the world, no matter how small.

Cat is convinced that his contribution – having a beautiful ass – constitutes living a worthwhile life. The fact that both Cat and Rimmer are judged worthy of life is not really a reflection of the Inquisitor's moral compass; they judged themselves, and as The Inquisitor puts it, 'by their own low standards, they have acquitted themselves'.

Because of his low self-worth and correspondingly low standards, Rimmer was judged to have done the best he could; Cat, who by his own argument is a pretty shallow guy, can also easily justify himself.

And while there is something to be said for doing your best to live a worthwhile life, if we judge 'best' and 'worthwhile' on purely self-imposed terms, we risk creating an entire culture as shallow and self-serving as Rimmer and the Cat.

On a purely human level, no matter how much we've squandered our lives, somehow we can always justify it – by our own screwed up values anyway.

Lister, on the other hand, knows there's more to life; we've seen him being the philosopher of the crew in many episodes. He could be more than a space bum, and he knows it – but he's lazy, and that's what gets him in trouble in the end.

But where it gets really interesting is with Kryten:

INQUISITOR: *Well, Kryten? Justify yourself.*
KRYTEN: *I'm not sure I can.*

INQUISITOR: *But surely your life is replete with good works? There can be few individuals who have lived a more selfless life.*

KRYTEN: *But I am programmed to live unselfishly. And therefore, any good works I do come not out of fine motives, but as a result of a series of binary commands I am compelled to obey.*

INQUISITOR: *Well, then, how can any mechanical justify himself?*

KRYTEN: *Perhaps only if he attempted to break his programming and conduct his life according to a set of values he arrived at independently.*

INQUISITOR: *Your argument invites deletion.*

KRYTEN: *The rules are yours, not mine.*

Taking Kryten's overall character arc I think there could be some holes made in this argument, but rather than debate that, let's just look at that conversation. If Kryten is selfless by programming only, his good works don't count. But if he were to break that programming and make his own choices, based on his own values... he would have to justify himself.

We've seen through Kryten's story that God could have programmed humans to be selfless and serve him and each other unquestioningly, but he chose instead to give us free will, so that our good works would be by choice and not some binary compulsion.

Because of that, we will also one day have to justify ourselves:

> *For we must all stand before Christ to be judged. We will each receive whatever we deserve for the good or evil we have done in this earthly body.*
>   *2 Cor 5:10 (NLT)*

So what's the answer?

Well, in the Red Dwarf universe, we would stand before the Inquisitor, and behind that mask we would not see him, but ourselves.

In a universe where God is real and is the ultimate judge of all, when we stand before him and he lifts his visor, we will not see ourselves; but God might see himself. If we accept that Christ is real, God – the Judge – will lift his visor and see not us, but his own Son.

You don't have to be a Saint, you don't have to be some great philanthropist, you don't have to be anything special; justification comes through faith alone, not through any amount of good work.

A simple carpenter's boy who learns how to do magic tricks like that and *doesn't* go into show business?

Do any of us believe that, even for a second?

– Rimmer, Holoship

Time Travelly Paradoxy Sci-fi Smeg

If I can go back and fix things so that I don't join the Space Corps, don't sign up with Red Dwarf, I can create an alternate existence, a NORMAL existence, back on Earth. I won't be stuck with your ugly mush for the next 3 million years.
  – Lister, Timeslides

In *Timeslides (S3 E5)*, Lister gets hold of some mutated photo developing fluid, some bubble wrap, and an idea that could get him back to Earth. An epic struggle between him and Rimmer ensues as both attempt to become disgustingly rich and famous...

Against all the odds, this works; Lister invents the Tension Sheet and becomes so rich he buys Buckingham Palace and has it ground down to line his drive.

And because Lister was directly responsible for Kryten and Cat joining the crew, Rimmer finds himself alone, 3 million years from Earth (despite the fact that Lister was also responsible for Rimmer's hologram being reactivated). Overlooking this minor plothole, Rimmer creates a time portal to Lister's mansion, where he tries to persuade Lister that being the last human in the universe, with only a smeg-head, a cat and a mechanoid for company, would be better than being a multi-multi-multi-millionaire who has to have sex with Lady Sabrina Mulholland-Jjones on a regular basis.

Rimmer fails spectacularly.

He does, however, attempt to show Lister's life for the shallow, empty existence we all want people like that to live, but when the only contrast he can offer is 'me with... with what I've got,' he is forced to concede that, of the two of them, Lister is in every way the richer man.

It is worth noting that both Lister and Thickie Holden, original inventor of the Tension Sheet, end up married to Lady Sabrina. Since the two seem to have little in common except being disgustingly rich and famous, perhaps Rimmer should have comforted himself with the knowledge that she had only married Lister for his money.

Of course, Rimmer doesn't realise this; instead he comes to the conclusion that being rich and famous is the solution to his multitude of problems.

In reality, 'lust for money brings trouble and nothing but trouble' (1 Tim 6:10 [MSG]), and while we don't see any down sides to Lister's billionaire lifestyle, Rimmer's jealousy of it ultimately brings them both down.

> *But men who want lots of money are tempted. They are trapped into doing all kinds of foolish things and things which hurt them. These things drag them into sin and will destroy them.*
> *1 Tim 6:9 (NLV)*

So Rimmer creates a time portal back to his dorm room at school, to persuade his (much) younger self to patent the Tension Sheet – apparently oblivious to the fact that Thickie Holden is right beside him and listening much more intently.

And so the timelines return to the way they started – the way they should be, because you can't change what has gone before. What has happened in the past just ends up part of life's journey; the experiences – the good, the bad and the ugly – that lead us to the place we are, as the people we are today. And more often than not, that is exactly who and where we are supposed to be, even if we don't feel like the richer man for it.

> *What about determinism, then? What about causality? You can't just mess about with history!*
> *– Holly, Timeslides*

So if we can't mess about with history, can we change the future?

The apparent conflict between predestination (the idea that God has already decided everything that will ever happen) and individual free will has been debated for centuries.

I will now demonstrate that all those theologians and scholars needed to do was crack open a can of Leopard Lager and watch *Future Echoes* (S1 E2), Red Dwarf's first experience with time travel, and an excellent place to examine the interaction of time travel, predestination and free will. And grammar.

LISTER: *Hey, it hasn't happened, has it? It has 'will have going to have happened' happened, but it hasn't actually 'happened' happened yet, actually.*

RIMMER: *Poppycock! It will be happened; it shall be going to be happening; it will be was an event that could will have been taken place in the future. Simple as that. Your bucket's been kicked, baby.*

The reason for this exchange is Rimmer witnessing a 'future echo' of Lister getting blown to pieces trying to fix the navicomp. Because he has seen it happen, Rimmer is convinced that his bunkmate's gory death must occur/have occurred in the future; in that way it is predestined.

Lister, meanwhile, is understandably less thrilled at the prospect of getting blown up, and sets about exercising his free will to change the next future echo – Cat breaking a tooth.

And so, when he realises that Cat is about to try and eat one of his electric goldfish (and likely break a tooth in the process), Lister rugby tackles Cat to stop him – resulting in a broken tooth.

The paradox here is that we can't know what would have happened if Lister had done nothing. Would Cat catch the fish? Would he still have broken a tooth? Would it have been the same tooth? And if not, does that mean Lister's action was predestined, and therefore not an act of free will?

What the Red Dwarf Posse realise, is that while Lister can exercise his free will, the best he can hope to do is change events leading up to a predestined event; he may change the cause, but the effect will remain the same.

Which is to say that certain events are predestined; like those things witnessed as future echoes, some things are planned by God and cannot be changed.

Take the example of Jonah. He had one job: to go to the city of Nineveh and tell the people that God had seen their sins and was done turning a blind eye.

(Jonah 1:2) This was the big picture event, the future echo that had to happen.

But Jonah refused, getting on a boat going the other way; then he got thrown overboard, spent three days in the naughty fish thinking about what he had done, got coughed up on a beach and finally went to Nineveh. This is the free will stuff, the variables.

(It's also worth noting that the people of Nineveh listened to Jonah and – of their own free will – stopped behaving like smegheads, and God's threatened doom was avoided. God must have known they would stop whatever it was he didn't like, but only when called out for it.)

The fact that some things are already decided – whether by God or by future echoes – doesn't affect our free will; but neither will our free will, ultimately, affect what God has already predestined.

Destiny – God's purpose – will be worked out, one way or another.

*

In *Cassandra* (S8 E4), the crew encounters a computer with the ability to unfailingly predict the future with 100% accuracy. Despite what they learned in Future Echoes, Rimmer still tries to cheat the future, and Lister, not liking the idea that his life is already planned out, flatly refuses to kill Cassandra – thus taking control of his destiny.

> *If the future's all worked out – horoscopes, all that stuff – it means we're not responsible for anything we do. It means we're just actors saying lines in a script written by someone else. I don't wanna believe that. I wanna believe I'm in charge of my own life, my own destiny; so I'm not gonna kill you, Cassandra. I'm out of here. Tomorrow's a new day. A fresh page in a book that's not been written yet. What happens in the future is up to me, not some 'predetermined destiny' smeg.*
> – Lister, Cassandra

By the end of the episode we have seen that Cassandra not only sees the future, but she also abuses this ability in order to manipulate the future for the Red Dwarf crew. Although she is unable to actively change the future, the information she feeds to the humans around her affects their actions. The actions are carried out entirely of the crew's own volition, but the outcomes are exactly as Cassandra saw – if not exactly as the crew interpreted her visions.

And maybe it's the same with free will and God's will. From his heavenly viewpoint somewhere outside of temporal existence he sees what will happen, drops whatever hints he considers necessary to nudge us in that direction, but always allows us to make the decision ourselves – and if we don't, he already knew that was a possibility, and had a Plan B ready to make things happen in some other way.

There are no surprises for God, and his purpose will find a way to happen.

*

From Lister's anguish out at being told how he will die, to Rimmer and Kochanski's opposite reactions to being told they will shortly be making love on the laundry room floor, our heroes have not had entirely rational responses to revelations about the future.

And maybe that's why Biblical prophecies tend to be symbolic, impersonal, even vague until they can be seen in hindsight.

In *Out of Time* (S6 E6) the Dwarfers discover another means to time travel, and witness what they will become: fat and middle class, seduced by power and wealth, they dispose of their morals and start hanging out with the Hitlers.

Even Rimmer, having seen this future, hates it so much that in an unusually heroic act he blows up Starbug, and the crew with it, to prevent it from happening.

And it doesn't.

In this instance, the future was not predetermined; what the crew saw was merely one possible future, a prophecy that wasn't intended to come true, but to serve as a warning of what could happen.

Maybe this was Rimmer's Nineveh moment, a last chance to change before being irretrievably doomed.

Backwards

In *Backwards* (S3 E1), Kryten and Rimmer disappear while on Kryten's flying test, and end up forming a novelty act on a planet which is, in fact, a version of late-1980s Earth where time runs backwards. This little thought experiment on the flow of time, while used here primarily for comic effect, can also throw out some interesting ideas about God and time, and more philosophical musings about whether life makes more sense in reverse.

For instance, Rimmer gives the example of Hitler, the hero who liberated Europe, while it falls to Lister to point out that Santa Claus is an organised crime boss.

By the same temporal logic, God is some kind of dictator who boots his friends out of paradise at the beginning of time, puts them through a lifetime on Earth, during which at some point they disown him, and repeats this throughout history until finally speaking the entirety of existence into oblivion.

Obviously, part of the fun in considering the existence of a 'backwards universe' is that it completely subverts everything we know about cause and effect.

So, in a world where St Francis of Assisi was a petty minded sadist, what does this mean for salvation?

Well, I'm going to suggest: nothing. There is only one act, and one decision, through which salvation is given. The act is the crucifixion of Christ. In our universe this act echoes backwards in time through Old Testament prophecy, and the salvation of the Israelites through faith in the promised Messiah, as well as forward to those of us lucky enough to be able to look back to a fixed point in time.

The decision is to believe in that act and accept the forgiveness offered by it. That forgiveness covers everything we have done up to that point, and everything we will do wrong from that point forward.

The exact point in time where each of these occurs has no effect on the salvation offered; nothing we can do can make us any more or less acceptable to God than our faith in Christ.

The Bible shows only one means of salvation: the grace of God, given to us through faith in Christ.

The only difference is that in our timeline we can read about the life and work of Jesus on Earth; in a backwards timeline the Old Testament Jews would have this, while we would have the more intangible hope of a Messiah yet to come.

The Bible is not specific about the relationship between God and Time. We don't know if he experiences time flowing in one direction as we do, or in both directions, or if everything effectively happens at once for God, and he can hop backwards and forwards through it at will.

If such a 'backwards dimension' were to exist, and assuming it is ruled over by the same God as our universe, this would appear to lend itself to a view of God as existing outside of time, with the ability to see both versions of the universe at once.

All we do know is that God 'inhabits eternity' (Isa 57:15), and that he planned our lives "before time began" (2 Tim 1:9; Titus 1:2) and "before the creation of the world" (Eph 1:4; 1 Peter 1:20 [NIV]).

Just as time is a nebulous and complex idea, God is far bigger and more complex; but as clocks and calendars bring the vastness of time down to a level where any human can have a basic understanding of it, so Jesus brought the vastness of God down to a human scale so that we all could understand him better.

A four-course meal of fear, vanity, guilt, and anger.

There are no aliens in the Red Dwarf universe. All the alien-esque creatures that feature in the show – Cat people, mechanoids, simulants, GELFs, figments of Lister's imagination... are all in some way created by humankind. In Red Dwarf, all of humanity's problems are of its own creation.

The absence of aliens is obviously something of a limitation for an ongoing science fiction show, so in the middle of series three we first encounter the primary workaround which would remain for the rest of the show's run – genetically engineered life forms (GELFs).

In *Polymorph* (S3 E3) we meet a genetic experiment gone wrong; a Giger-esque monster with more teeth than the entire Osmond family and the ability to shapeshift at will, which feeds off the negative emotions of its prey.

This is the first time we get to see the crew playing different versions of themselves, as the Polymorph pushes each crew member to the limit of his worst emotion and then sucks it right out of his forehead (even a mechanoid with no emotions and a hologram with no forehead, but we're not here to go plotholing).

Through this we can see just how the characters are shaped by their emotions: Lister becomes fearless and just wants to rip out the monster's windpipe and beat it to death with the tonsil end, while Rimmer turns into a goatee wearing hippy and sets himself up as some sort of peace envoy. Cat finds a gutter somewhere and falls over drunk, while Kryten is quite happy to just hand the others over and do a runner while the monster is busy eating them alive.

Lister loses his fear; Cat loses his vanity; Kryten loses his guilt, and Rimmer his anger.

On the one hand, Polymorph is an Alien homage with jokes. On the other, it's a lesson in how the negative aspects of our personality affect who we are, for better or worse.

Fear, anger, guilt, vanity… as we know, these are all things which lead to the dark side, so why does God allow them to carry on in his followers?

Well, maybe he allows us to be fearful so we won't end up sacrificing our lives in some stupid pointless way.

Maybe he lets us get angry because there are some things in life that can't be reasoned with, and we just need to face them head on.

Maybe he allows us to be vain because the opposite – a complete lack of self-worth – would be more damaging.

Maybe he makes us feel guilt because, at some point in our lives, we put a bazookoid to his back and fed him to the mutant.

Maybe it's ok to have and to express emotions – even the 'bad' ones.

*

There is a Biblical meaning of fear, specifically used in reference to fearing God, which doesn't mean he is a chameleonic monster waiting to drain us of our emotions; it means we should be aware of his power, and respectful of his authority.

Even this kind of fear, rather than the running away terrified kind, might have prevented Lister doing anything stupid in the face of the polymorph.

God merely wants us to have the right kind of fear, for the right kind of things; if he had wanted us to suffer hippopotomonstrosesquippedaliophobia he wouldn't have told Isaiah to name his son Mahershalalhashbaz (Isaiah 8:1).

Anger, too, is ok if handled correctly:

> *If you are angry, do not let it become sin. Get over your anger before the day is finished.*
> *Eph 4:26 (NLV)*

Jesus never faced a shape-shifting GELF, but there were times when being meek and mild didn't cut it, and he had to declare clobbering time:

> Jesus went straight to the Temple and threw out everyone who had set up shop, buying and selling. He kicked over the tables of loan sharks and the stalls of dove merchants. He quoted this text: My house was designated a house of prayer; You have made it a hangout for thieves.
> Matt 21:12-13 (MSG)

Jesus here is demonstrating the right way to get angry; it's not personal, he is angry on behalf of the victims of injustice, and especially that such injustice is taking place in the temple. And he leaves his anger there; he doesn't bear a grudge.

And this is important; bearing a grudge is shown to be a significant issue for Rimmer in *Trojan* (S10 E1), when a quantum rod causes him to come into contact with his brother Howard (also now a hologram). The millennia-old resentment Rimmer feels for his better looking, more successful brothers is awakened again, and manifests itself in the form of self-created malware, which overloads his brain and crashes his light bee.

In order to reinstate Rimmer, Kryten performs a resentment drain, after which we get a momentary glimpse of a more pleasant Rimmer who has realised that competing with his brother won't make him happy. Rimmer's head feels emptier – unburdened – without his resentment.

For a moment, we see what he could be if he would just man up and forgive his brothers for the perceived wrong they have done toward him; and a perceived wrong is exactly what it turns out to be, when Howard is also affected by a resentment overload, caused by his jealousy of Arnold's (albeit faked) success.

Unlike his brother, however, Howard's change seems to go deeper, to the extent that he willingly takes a bullet for Arnold, and then makes a deathbed confession that he is, in fact, just a vending machine repair man.

And when it comes right down to it, isn't that all any of us are? We are all flawed, imperfect human beings; and we should all be open to the possibility that we are somebody's Howard. We may not be able to do anything about our Arnold, but we can make a start by letting go of our own resentments. By forgiving our Howards, and being honest about our own faults, we can receive a resentment drain and be released from the burden of bitterness.

But I'll tell you whom to fear. Fear God, who has the power to kill you and then throw you into hell. Yes, he's the one to fear.

Luke 12:5 NLT

We have nothing to fear but fear itself. Apart from pain. And maybe humiliation and obviously death. And failure. But apart from fear, pain and humiliation, failure and the unknown and death we have nothing to fear but fear itself.

– *Rimmer, The Beginning*

Blubbery Schoolgirl Mush

Thanks For The Memory (S2 E3) is another of those occasions scattered through Red Dwarf's history where Rimmer becomes a slightly more agreeable character, this time celebrating his deathday with his crewmates on the surface of a convenient planet. After getting him hologramatically drunk, Lister and the Cat discover what was missing from Rimmer's life to make him such a total smeghead:

> *I'd trade it all in – all of it. My pips, my long-service medals, my swimming certificates, my telescope, my shoe trees. I'd trade everything in to be loved and to have been loved.*

And so, in a fit of drunken benevolence, Lister attempts to heal Rimmer's brokenness by giving him the memories of an eight month love affair with Lise Yates. As Rimmer recalls that strange summer he inexplicably spent in Liverpool, he is subconsciously schooled in the ups and downs of love. He learns what happens if we take a risk now and then: sometimes we get hurt, sometimes we start drinking and smoking for no good reason, but we also learn, and grow, and have the chance to become a better person.

And with the experience of being in love now firmly embedded in his mind, Rimmer is... nice. At least, until that inevitable moment when he discovers what has happened, and insists that Lister undoes it.

In the memory of Lise Yates, Lister gives Rimmer the vital ingredient his life has been missing, the one thing that could raise him above being a complete git all the time: love.

And Rimmer hands it right back.

*

Having deliberately forgotten Lise Yates, Rimmer once again becomes sceptical about love, and at the beginning of *Holoship* (S5 E1) an old romantic movie elicits this response:

RIMMER: *Those kind of films really irritate me. Just not realistic. There isn't a man in the universe who wouldn't have taken the job and to hell with the woman. Total baloney.*

LISTER: *Rimmer, you said that about "King of Kings – the story of Jesus!"*

RIMMER: *Well, it's true! A simple carpenter's son who learns how to do magic tricks like that and doesn't go into show-business? Do any of us believe that, even for a second?*

LISTER: *He was supposed to be the Son of God.*

And it is at about this point that the boys encounter the Holoship Enlightenment and its crew of dead geniuses – which, having convinced Captain Hercule Platini that that he has been in command of Red Dwarf for nearly four years, Rimmer is permitted to join – provided he can get better exam marks than an existing crew member.

Being, well, not a genius, the only hope Rimmer has of passing the test, getting on board Enlightenment, and pursuing his dream of becoming a 'somebody' is by undergoing an illegal, immoral, and highly dangerous mind patch in order to access a greater intellect than his own.

However, the mind patch fails because deep down Rimmer still sees himself as hopeless; his brain won't accept good things happening to him and rejects the mind patch. Holoship crew member Nirvanah Crane, having taken leave of her senses and fallen in love with Arnie, can see through that though:

> *Underneath all that neurotic mess is someone nice trying to get out. Someone who deserves a chance to grow. So, you won't give up, OK?*

And on that note, Crane effectively gives up her hologramatic existence so that Rimmer can live his best life – bringing us full circle back to the carpenter's son mentioned in the opening scene.

And among that carpenter's son's magic tricks is the ability to see through our neurotic messes to the someone nice – to the 'somebody' we are deep down. All it took for Rimmer to become somebody was to be loved – loved enough that someone would give up their life for him to achieve his dream. Rimmer grasped that, and gave everything back. He grew, and was a better man.

*

Choosing a life following Christ is just as much a rollercoaster. Less so here in England than in many other places, but it does demand personal sacrifice. It needs an occasional 'unpopular' decision to be made. It may even need you to move to Liverpool.

It certainly isn't all sunshine all of the time, but it does bring a love that will change us more profoundly – and more permanently – than eight months of stupendous sex with Lise Yates. That love is offered to us as a gift – to accept and let it change us from the inside, or to hand back and forget it ever existed.

Learning to love, and learning to be loved, makes Rimmer feel better about himself, and as a result, he is a nicer person to be around; and that's just from the love of another human being.

God is love (1 John 4:7-21), and we are called to "Be imitators of God ... and live a life of love" (Eph. 5:1–2 [NIV]).

Holoship Rimmer ends up repaying Nirvanah Crane with his own sacrifice, preferring to give up his dreams of becoming a somebody on the Enlightenment for the knowledge that the woman he loves, and more importantly who loves him, is still out there somewhere.

He hasn't always been so noble, of course; in *White Hole* (S4 E4), he was granted a reprieve because there would be insufficient power to reboot him from the emergency batteries, despite the fact that without his drain on the system, Lister and Cat could extend their (admittedly still very short) remaining time. Under such circumstances, Space Corps Directives dictate that 'a hologramatic crewmember must lay down his life in order that the living crewmembers might survive'.

Rimmer can – and being a stickler for rules, should – make the ultimate sacrifice here, and lay down his life so that what passes as his friends can live longer. But of course he would rather refuse, even if this means watching them die, and then carrying on, alone, until he eventually runs out of power and 'dies' anyway.

Compare and contrast this with Lister, who despite being unable to sacrifice his guitar to save his own life in *Marooned* (S3 E2), was willing to gamble his own safety for a mere android in *The Last Day* (S3 E6).

And in *Terrorform* (S5 E3) the others collectively put themselves at risk to rescue Rimmer from his own self-loathing – all Rimmer needed to do in order to escape his inner demons was to believe that his crewmates liked him and wanted him around.

You don't need to be a believer to see that 'There is no greater love than to lay down one's life for one's friends' (John 15:13 [NLT]), a truth which was ultimately fulfilled when Jesus was willing to gamble his own safety for a mere human; to love us enough for our demons to run and hide.

Humans, meanwhile, tend to be more like Cat, who in Give & Take (S11 E3) faces the trivial question of whether to give up a kidney for the man who is, essentially, his God. (I like to think there is a tiny part of him that wants to do this, but struggles to be heard over his vain and selfish facade – again, a lot like us in many ways.)

If you go through life without feeling, if you go through life never experiencing, you're no better than a jellyfish. No better than a bank manager.

– *Rimmer, Thanks For The Memory*

If I have the gift of prophecy and can fathom all mysteries and all knowledge, and if I have a faith that can move mountains, but do not have love, I am nothing.

1 Cor 13:2 (NIV)

I think I E5 A9 08 B7 you

It's the old, old story. Droid meets droid. Droid becomes chameleon. Droid loses chameleon, chameleon becomes blob, droid gets blob back again. It's a classic tale.
    – Kryten, Camille

In *Camille* (S4 E1) it's Kryten who has his shot at true love when he rescues a female shaped mechanoid going by the name of Camille.

When Rimmer meets Camille, we don't really know what is going on, but it doesn't take Lister long to realise something weird is going on, and to force a confession: that Camille is a pleasure GELF – a genetically engineered life form created to be everyone's perfect companion; a mirror for their obsessions.

Rimmer, Lister and Cat are content – while it lasts – to fall for the act, to see (and flirt with) Camille as their perfect mate. But with her true identity revealed, it transpires that Camille has genuine feelings toward Kryten, who gallantly lies about Camille's bum looking blobby in her natural state, and even takes her on a date as herself.

The moral of which is that appearance is not everything; what we are is more than what we look like, more than the way we appear to those around us.

Indeed, whether we know it or not, like Camille we are probably projecting some image of ourselves to those we meet with, depending on the situation and our relationship with the individuals involved.

It took someone pure, someone programmed to be 'good', to see beyond outward appearances and see Camille's heart – and as a result, Kryten is able to give up his best shot at true E5 A9 08 B7, and do what is best for Camille, however much it hurts him.

Just as Camille cannot hide her true self, or what she truly needs, from someone who truly loves her, neither can we hide ourselves from God. You can make yourself look like a fun-loving working class scouser, or an ambitious but rubbish wannabe officer, or whatever else any given situation demands, but God sees through that and not only sees your inner blob, but loves it and will give it exactly what it needs.

> The LORD does not look at the things people look at. People look at the outward appearance, but the LORD looks at the heart.
> 1 Samuel 16:7 (NIV)

Wasn't it St. Francis of Assisi himself who said 'Never give a sucker an even break'?

– *Rimmer, Holoship*

If we're not who we thought we were, who the hell are we?

At the end of Series 5, *Back to Reality* presents a dramatic plot twist in which we discover that our heroes have really just been hiding in a total immersion video game for four years because, as Sebastian 'Lister' Doyle puts it, 'Either we're running away from god-knows-what, or we have nothing worth living for in the first place.'

As they try to become accustomed to their 'real' personalities, it becomes increasingly clear that our heroes are all what they – within the game – have come to hate most:

Rimmer is a scruffy hobo named Billy Doyle whose cologne is "Eau de Yak Urine".

Even worse, he can no longer blame this on his parents, because he shared an upbringing with a richer, more important, half-brother Sebastian – who also happens to be the mass-murdering Voter-Colonel of a totalitarian state, in contrast to the morally upright Dave Lister.

Cat has lost his 'cool', and is so mind-meltingly shallow that life as Duane Dibbley has no meaning.

And Kryten is tested to the point of taking a human life.

Each of these things is the polar opposite of what our heroes have come to see as their defining characteristics; so much so that they are each driven to suicidal depths of despair.

But of course, these are alter-egos, created specifically to induce despair; the characters we know and love have been deceived into seeing themselves as undeserving of life.

They become convinced that they are uncool, worthless, evil.

And yet…

And yet, that is not, and never has been, their true identity.

You may find your identity in your social class, or your job, or the way you look (or smell!). You may find it in the things you have done, the way you have spent your life, however good or bad that may be. For most of us our identity is, in some way, caught up in how other people see us.

And yet…

And yet, that is not, and never has been, your true identity.

You are not your job; you're not your parents, and you're definitely not your siblings. You're not your bank balance, or the car you drive.

You're not the results of that 'Which Red Dwarf character are you' quiz you did on the internet last week. And you are not your past sins.

All of those are alter-egos, designed to distract us from who we really are; a manufactured appearance to disguise the ugly reality.

In Back to Reality, Holly has to find a way to break through the shared hallucination and communicate with Kryten, to bring the Dwarfers back to who they really are.

And in our reality, God is trying to break through the illusions and distractions this world throws at us, to try and bring us back to our true identity – not as a hideous blob, but as he sees us: as children of God.

Your Father is Dad

Lister drifted through life because, being an orphan, he has never had any real sense of identity; he doesn't know where he came from, or who he is – until he discovers the meaning of *Ourobouros* (S7 E3). Thanks to some more 'time-travelly, paradoxy, sci-fi smeg', Lister becomes his own father, creating a self-sustaining feedback loop of last humans, allowing humanity to go on forever.

Lister's father, although invisible throughout most of his life, turns out to have been closer than he could have ever imagined. And once he realises this, Lister can move on, knowing he wasn't really abandoned, but placed on earth for a purpose – to maintain the unbreakable circle, to keep the human race from dying out.

Unfortunately, these circumstances mean that Lister grew up without a solid father figure, and is therefore not a great father himself – something he tries to make amends for in *Fathers & Suns* (S10 E2).

Rimmer, on the other hand, is constantly reminding his crewmates that his neuroses are largely down to his overambitious father, who failed to make the Space Corps and pursued his dreams vicariously through his sons.

Despite the physical, mental and emotional abuse that followed, Rimmer was desperate to earn his father's respect, and his inability to do so only added to his own disappointment in himself.

His father's disapproval becomes a demon which haunts Rimmer throughout his life (and death), as Cat points out in *The Beginning* (S10 E6), as the crew is about to be obliterated by Simulant Death Ships.

This should be Rimmer's 'moment of destiny'; the point to which all his obsessive General-worship and Risk campaigning has been leading. Reluctantly, he accepts the responsibility and takes the chance to prove himself, but is unable to concentrate long enough to formulate a battle plan.

At Cat's prompting, Rimmer decides that the only way to clear his head is to exorcise the demon: to play a holographic message from his father, which he was given to play when he eventually became an officer, or a 'somebody'.

And that is when everything changes. After finally watching the message, Rimmer stops feeling like he has failed, stops trying to impress his father by being someone he obviously wasn't meant to be. All because he hears this:

> *Arnold, I'm not your father. Look inside yourself and you will know I speak the truth. Your father wasn't me... it's Dungo, our gardener.*
> *Rimmer's father, The Beginning*

Rimmer has always dreamt of being 'somebody'. In his own eyes, he was a failure because he defined himself by his job of Chicken Soup Nozzle Repairman, despite Lister telling him that was just a job, and Kryten reminding him that Albert Einstein was not just a clerk in a patent office.

Rimmer sees himself as a failure because he is constantly comparing himself to his brothers in an effort to earn his father's approval.

But he's not John, or Howard, or Frank; none of us are. We are all ourselves, uniquely created and accepted just the way we are, with our own skills, our own flaws, our own ambitions, our own favourite episode of Red Dwarf. God made you intentionally, not to be a carbon copy of your least favourite sibling, but to be you.

Only when Rimmer discovers that his father was somebody else – somebody who had entirely different expectations of him and would have been proud of who Arnold Rimmer actually was – can he stop trying to be someone else, and be truly himself.

And once he sees himself as his real father would see him, Arnold Rimmer finds a new sense of self-worth, sucks it up, and finally acts like the senior officer on board – not only coming up with a daring escape plan, but sticking to his guns when the others declare it to be crap, and getting them to pull together behind it.

*

Our heroes have very different experiences, but both have been negatively impacted by the father figures in their lives.

Which brings more questions: where Rimmer blamed his father for his failures, who can Lister blame? Is the mess Lister made of his life his own fault, or can he blame his father? If your Dad is a total bum (or as

Lister might have it, a bum, but not a total bum), or an authoritarian, how does that affect your view of God as a Father?

Can we as Christians blame our heavenly father if we make a mess of our lives? Does he want to exercise tough love and throw our beloved guitar out of the airlock? Or will he, in fact, throw us out of the airlock if necessary?

Regardless of whether you had a great Dad, or an emotionless authoritarian like Rimmer's, or an absentee father like Lister, sometimes we all need to remember that we have another Father, and to think about what he wants and expects from us, and how he feels about us even when those around us seem to think we are worthless.

Once we know who our Father is, we can begin to get a sense of who we really are – and once we start trying to be that person, instead of whoever we think other people want us to be, that's when we can make a difference to the world around us.

More Than Just a Toaster

A variation on this idea can be seen in *Give & Take* (S11 E3), where Kryten mistakes a Robby the Robot lookalike for the superior medi-bot Asclepius, and has it taken back to Red Dwarf.

Back on the Dwarf, having dispensed a lengthy and productive session of therapy for Rimmer, it eventually transpires that the retro-styled robot should in fact have been dispensing nothing more medical than a can of Dr Pepper.

Nonetheless, the boys from the Dwarf convince Snacky that he's not just a snack dispenser any more; he has learnt more than he realizes, and as a result has new potential – potential which, in a roundabout sort of way, helps them to save Lister (who now has less kidney than a chip shop pie).

> *You're just a snack dispenser if you think you're just a snack dispenser but you're not only a snack dispenser you're something more if you decide you want to be something more...*
> *– Rimmer, Give & Take*

Like Snacky, we don't always see the best of ourselves. We don't always see beyond our perceived identity as a snack vendor, or an estate agent, or a patent clerk, and we fail to see that we actually have the potential to save lives, or run a country, or whatever it is we're meant to do.

Snacky was made in the image of Robby the Robot, but when he realised he was more than just a snack dispenser, he made a difference to the Red Dwarf

Posse. Each of us is made in the image of God… imagine what we can achieve when we accept this fact.

It just strikes me that there might be something more. Something greater. Something unimaginably more splendid than heating bread.
    – Talkie Toaster, Waiting for God

Like Snacky, Talkie Toaster is all too aware of his lot in life: his sole purpose is to furnish his owner with hot, buttered, scrummy toast. After an 18 day run of Lister not wanting toast, Talkie is, understandably, starting to question the meaning of life. If Lister doesn't want toast, Talkie's life is meaningless; and being artificially intelligent, he is able to consider alternative vocations.

Unfortunately for Talkie, the path to something greater consists of being smashed to pieces by Lister and later reassembled by Kryten for experimental purposes…

We can only hope that our own search for purpose is less dramatic, but even if we do end up in life's garbage hold in three thousand separate pieces, there is always hope; our God is in the business of healing broken people, and can pick you up and rebuild you, ready for some new and unimaginably more splendid purpose.

*

God doesn't want you to simply be you; you already are. He wants you to be the best possible you; you on the right brand of vitamins, not just on the really good days, but every day.

God wants us to be us from Dimension Jump (S4 E5). He wants Spanners, a more talented and popular version of Lister, who has become a Space Corps technician and married Kochanski; he wants a human version of Cat whose early religious education led him to become a Chaplain.

He wants Commander 'Ace' Rimmer.

In *Stoke Me a Clipper* (S7 E2) we saw Ace return to recruit our Rimmer as his replacement. But before that can happen, Arnold has to stop fighting Ace, look beyond his own flaws and see what he can become.

And when he does, he becomes even more himself (on a really good day).

As the new Ace, Rimmer has a purpose; a life he was created to live, but couldn't until he believed he was Ace. And like Rimmer, we have a new identity and a new purpose waiting; as a believer in Christ, you are a new creation, alive in Christ and loved by God. In his eyes, you are Ace.

We all have that potential, an Ace inside us waiting to be released. It's not always easy to accept ourselves – the good and the bad – but until we do that we may not find the particular part of ourselves that we are meant to fully become.

Just as Ace took the cowardly snivelling Arnold Rimmer under his wing, God accepts us at our weakest, and builds us up into the best we can be.

It may take some false starts to figure out who you're supposed to be, but once you do, you can be a better you. Or as philosopher and theologian Howard Thurman said much more succinctly than a mere author like me ever could:

> *Don't ask yourself what the world needs. Ask yourself what makes you come alive, and then go do that. Because what the world needs is people who have come alive.*

Who knows, you may even discover your inner Ace. Smoke me a kipper…

Demons and Angels

LISTER: *Can you be two things simultaneously?*
KRYTEN: *Take you, sir. In some ways you're bright, sensitive and caring. In other ways you're an irresponsible, curry-obsessed moron.*
– Tikka to Ride (Xtended)

In *Demons & Angels* (S5 E5) a Triplicator malfunction creates 'high' and 'low' versions of the ship and crew. The Highs represent their spiritual side, their ultimate potential; whereas the Lows are comprised solely of that part of them that likes horror movies, violence and meaningless sex.

It's possible to extrapolate from the crew we know to the Low equivalents we meet in this episode: a malfunctioning Kryten acting with no inhibitions and a devolved, sabre-toothed Cat, while low Lister thrives on mindless violence, and Rimmer on sexual perversion. (Of course there is nothing inherently wrong with steak, sex and slasher-flicks in and of themselves; what we see in the Lows could be considered the result of excessive misuse of those things.)

The Highs, on the other hand, bear little resemblance to the original crew; this possibly points to a lack of definitive spiritual direction on the part of the writers, but if our highest potential is to become part of an amorphous group of soul siblings with no discernible individuality – not to mention common sense – I don't think I want it, thanks.

The Highs appear to be defined by the (unbiblical) proverb 'too heavenly minded for any earthly good'; High Kryten is unable to see the Lows as inherently bad, and all of them are compelled to help the Lows at any cost.

While this could be argued to be a positive trait in the real world – the episode hinges on the fact that there is good and bad in everyone, after all – their apparent obliviousness to the existence of evil leads very quickly to the bloody death of two of their number.

And so we come back to Lister's question: can you be two things simultaneously? Do both extremes really exist within us? In Demons and Angels it's Lister who provides the metaphor, when he – the original, baseline Lister – is literally controlled by his Low self, and forced against his will to kill his High self.

And that, on some level, is the struggle we all face: our evil nature is always lurking, waiting for an opportunity to take control, and make us do something to kill off our High self, our potential.

So what can we do about it?

*

In *Tikka to Ride* (S7 E1) the Posse head back in time to top up on curry supplies, but inadvertently prevent the assassination of JFK – leading to the fall of the USA, the Space Corps never being founded, and the non-existence of Red Dwarf.

Reviewing the history books, Kryten explains how JFK was both good and bad – both a liberal icon, and an inveterate womaniser. Kryten compares this to himself, having disabled his guilt chip and discarded his behaviour protocols.

We all have the potential to be bright, sensitive and caring; or to be an irresponsible, curry-obsessed moron. In the Bible, the apostle Paul puts this choice in very stark terms:

> *So kill your earthly impulses: loose sex, impure actions, unbridled sensuality, wicked thoughts, and greed.*
> *Col 3:5 (VOICE)*

In Tikka to Ride, Lister presents JFK with an even more direct choice:

> *Where I come from you're a liberal icon, and that's the person you should be. If you're gonna be that person, you're gonna have to sacrifice your life.*
> *– Lister, Tikka to Ride*

In the altered timeline, Low JFK was left unchecked, and brought the world to the brink of nuclear war; to prevent this, JFK literally kills his earthly impulses by assassinating the version of himself which embodies them. He sacrifices himself to become, in the history books at least, High JFK.

Luckily, we don't have to find a time wand and murder our earlier, sinful selves; we can assassinate our 'bad' self by accepting Jesus and letting him die in our place:

> *We know that our old life, our old sinful self, was nailed to the cross with Christ. And so the power of sin that held us was destroyed. Sin is no longer our boss.*
> *Rom 6:6 (NLV)*

That way, like JFK, we can be reborn as a better version of ourselves.

Mister Jesus?

He hath risen!

– Kryten, Lemons

The Beginning: Better Than Life

The new sensation sweeping the solar system is the total immersion video game, "Better Than Life." Using the new senso-lock feedback technology, "Better Than Life" is able to detect all your desires and fantasies and then make them come true.
  – Newsreader, Better Than Life

As a final thought, we'll go back to series 2, where, on the way back towards Earth, our heroes encounter a mail pod which has been tracking Red Dwarf through the millennia.

Here they discover that Rimmer's tax bill is massive and his father is dead; thankfully, they also find a copy of the total immersion video game 'Better Than Life' with which to take his mind off things.

This was way back in 1988, when the exciting potential of blocky 'virtual reality' worlds presented by oversized goggles and interacted with by gloves was the very pinnacle of computer technology; the hardware is similar, but when Cat and Lister boot up the game they find themselves in a much more realistic and immersive virtual world.

Once inside the game, almost any fantasy they can conjure up is available to them. Lister and Cat are content with a round of golf, caviar vindaloo and a mermaid girlfriend; meanwhile Rimmer becomes an

Admiral in the Space Corps, sharing port and cigars with the Field Marshal and various other hoity-toity gimboids.

And there is nothing at all wrong with using a video game, or a movie, or a sci-fi sitcom, for a couple of hours of escapism from the unpleasant realities of everyday life. Nobody could blame the boys for wanting to escape the pressures of being the last human, grieving lost loved ones, and the ever present threat of unpayable bills.

It would be nice to think that being chummy with God would mean that we're protected from bad things; unfortunately the truth is that both death and taxes are still inevitable, and that various other unpleasant things still happen to Christians. What we need to do is be mindful of how we choose to deal with them; running away from our problems and hiding in a computer game (or wherever suits us better) will invariably turn sour.

In the TV episode *Better Than Life* (S2 E2), the only down side is that Rimmer's subconscious can't accept nice things happening to him, and he fantasises himself and his crewmates into ever worsening situations.

In the second Red Dwarf novel, also called *Better Than Life*, the negative effects of the game are explored in much more detail, as the near perfect artificial reality becomes highly addictive, and as socially and physically harmful as any drug. (Again quite prescient for 1988, before the worldwide web, mobile devices and internet addictions.)

From the Christian perspective, we all have access to something far better than this life – we just need to allow ourselves to become totally immersed in God. After all, he knows your true desires better than any senso-lock feedback technology could hope to, and has the ultimate power to make them happen.

> *Enjoy serving the LORD, and he will give you what you want.*
> *Psalm 37:4 (NCV)*

> *I came so they can have real and eternal life, more and better life than they ever dreamed of.*
> *John 10:10 (MSG)*

This decision could completely alter the whole course of your life.

Mrs Rimmer, Dimension Jump

www.ingramcontent.com/pod-product-compliance
Lightning Source LLC
Chambersburg PA
CBHW031419290426
44110CB00011B/448